THE UNHOLY CRUSADE

✒ THE LOCHLAINN SEABROOK COLLECTION ✒

Five-Star Books & Gifts From the Heart of the American South

✒ SeaRavenPress.com ✒

THE UNHOLY

LINCOLN'S LEGACY OF DESTRUCTION IN THE AMERICAN SOUTH

A PICTORIAL STUDY

Illustrated by the author, Colonel

LOCHLAINN SEABROOK

JEFFERSON DAVIS HISTORICAL GOLD MEDAL WINNER

Diligently Researched for the Elucidation of the Reader

2017

Sea Raven Press, Nashville, Tennessee, USA

THE UNHOLY CRUSADE

Published by
Sea Raven Press, Cassidy Ravensdale, President
The Literary Wing of the Pro-South Movement
PO Box 1484, Spring Hill, Tennessee 37174-1484 USA
SeaRavenPress.com • searavenpress@gmail.com

Sea Raven Press

Enlightening, educational, & entertaining books for the whole family!

1st SRP paperback edition, 1st printing: January 2017, ISBN: 978-1-943737-39-0
1st SRP hardcover edition, 1st printing: January 2017, ISBN: 978-1-943737-41-3

ISBN: 978-1-943737-39-0 (paperback)
Library of Congress Control Number: 2016962202

The Unholy Crusade: Lincoln's Legacy of Destruction in the American South, by Lochlainn Seabrook.
Includes an index, endnotes, and bibliographical references. Written in 2016, published in 2017.

Front and back cover design and art, book design, layout, and interior art by Lochlainn Seabrook.
All images, graphic design, graphic art, and illustrations copyright © Lochlainn Seabrook.
Cover image & design copyright © Lochlainn Seabrook.
Cover photo: City ruins, Richmond Virginia, April 1865
Portions of this book have been adapted from the author's other works

The views on the American "Civil War" documented in this book are those of the publisher.

The paper used in this book is acid-free and lignin-free. It has been certified by the Sustainable Forestry
Initiative and the Forest Stewardship Council and meets all ANSI standards for archival quality paper.

PRINTED & MANUFACTURED IN OCCUPIED TENNESSEE, FORMER CONFEDERATE STATES OF AMERICA

Dedication

To those of my Confederate ancestors who were burned out of their homes and murdered by Yankee troops. We will not let your memory be forgotten.

Epigraph

"If these fanatics [Northern Liberals] ever get the power in their own hands they will override the Constitution, set the Supreme Court at defiance, change and make laws to suit themselves, lay violent hands on them who differ in opinion, or who dare question their fidelity, and finally deluge the country with blood."

Daniel Webster, 1850

CONTENTS

SEA RAVEN PRESS

THE WORLD'S #1 SOUTH-FRIENDLY BOOK PUBLISHER

Restoring Dixie's honor
Defending traditional Southern culture
Preserving authentic Confederate history
One book at a time!

Nashville, Tennessee

SeaRavenPress.com

NOTES TO THE READER

THE TWO MAIN POLITICAL PARTIES IN 1860

☛ In any study of America's antebellum, bellum, and postbellum periods, it is vitally important to understand that in 1860 the two major political parties—the Democrats and the newly formed Republicans—were the opposite of what they are today. In other words, the Democrats of the mid 19th Century were Conservatives, akin to the Republican Party of today, while the Republicans of the mid 19th Century were Liberals, akin to the Democratic Party of today.[1]

In fact, the modern Republican Party—a political descendant of the progressive 18th-Century Federalist Party—was founded in 1854 by liberals (then sometimes known as "fusionists") familiar with communist Karl Marx,[2] who along with various types of socialists, radicals, and revolutionaries, wrote its platform, served as delegates at the 1860 Republican convention, zealously campaigned for Lincoln,[3] and were instrumental in getting him into the White House.[4]

The author's cousin, Confederate Vice President and Democrat Alexander H. Stephens: a Southern Conservative.

In essence then the Confederacy's Democratic president, Jefferson Davis, was a Conservative (with libertarian leanings); the Union's Republican president, Abraham Lincoln, was a Liberal (with socialistic leanings). This is why, in the mid 1800s, the conservative wing of the Democratic Party was known as "the States' Rights Party,"[5] it is why Lincoln idolized the radical leaders of the European socialist revolution of 1848,[6] and it is why the radical left members of the Republican Party agreed with socialists and communists that the American "Civil War" was a "revolutionary movement" (Marx), a "radical revolution" (Thaddeus Stevens), and a "social revolution" (James A. Garfield).[7]

Hence, the Democrats of the Civil War period referred to themselves as "conservatives," "confederates," "anti-centralists," or "constitutionalists" (the latter because they favored rigorous adherence to the original Constitution—which tacitly guaranteed states' rights—as created by the Founding Fathers), while the Republicans called themselves "liberals," "nationalists," "centralists," or "consolidationists" (the latter three because they wanted to nationalize the central government and consolidate political power in Washington, D.C.).[8] Due to the 19th-Century Republicans' (Liberals') hatred of the Constitution (which they derogatorily referred to as a "scrap of paper"),[9] Democrats (Conservatives) of that era called them "radicals,"[10] or more accurately, the "Anti-Constitutional Party."[11]

Since in our post-truth political world these facts are new to most of my readers,[12] let us further demystify them by viewing them from the perspective of the American Revolutionary War. If Davis and his *conservative* Southern constituents (the Democrats of 1861) had been alive in 1775, they would have sided with George Washington and the American colonists, who sought to secede from the tyrannical government of Great Britain; if Lincoln and his *liberal* Northern constituents (the Republicans of 1861) had been alive at that time, they would have sided with King George III and the English monarchy, who sought to maintain the American colonies as possessions of the British Empire. It is due to this very comparison that Southerners often refer to the "Civil War" as the

U.S. President William McKinley, in 1896 the first Conservative Republican since the party's inception in 1854.

Second American Revolutionary War.

Without a basic understanding of these facts, the American "Civil War" will forever remain incomprehensible. For more on this topic see my book, *Abraham Lincoln Was a Liberal, Jefferson Davis Was a Conservative: The Missing Key to Understanding the American Civil War.*

THE TERM "CIVIL WAR"

☛ As I heartily dislike the phrase "Civil War," its use throughout this book (as well as in my other works) is worthy of an explanation.

Today America's entire literary system refers to the conflict of 1861 using the Northern term the "Civil War," whether we in the South like it or not. Thus, as all book searches by readers, libraries, and retail outlets are now performed online, and as all bookstores categorize works from this period under the heading "Civil War," book publishers and authors who deal with this particular topic have little choice but to use this term themselves. If I were to refuse to use it, as some of my Southern colleagues have suggested, few people would ever find or read my books.

The American "Civil War" was not a true civil war as Webster defines it: "A conflict between opposing groups of citizens of the *same* country." It was a fight between two individual countries; or to be more specific, two separate and constitutionally formed confederacies: the U.S.A. and the C.S.A.

Add to this the fact that scarcely any non-Southerners have ever heard of the names we in the South use for the conflict, such as the "War for Southern Independence"—or my personal preference, "Lincoln's War." It only makes sense then to use the term "Civil War" in most commercial situations, distasteful though it is.

We should also bear in mind that while today educated persons, particularly educated Southerners, all share an abhorrence for the phrase "Civil War," it was not always so. Confederates who lived through and even fought in the conflict regularly used the term throughout the 1860s, and even long after. Among them were Confederate generals such as

Nathan Bedford Forrest, Richard Taylor, and Joseph E. Johnston, not to mention the Confederacy's vice president, Alexander H. Stephens.

In 1895 Confederate General James Longstreet wrote about his military experiences in a work subtitled, *Memoirs of the Civil War in America*. Even the Confederacy's highest leader, President Jefferson Davis, used the term "Civil War,"[13] and in one case at least, as late as 1881—the year he wrote his brilliant exposition, *The Rise and Fall of the Confederate Government*.[14] Authors writing for *Confederate Magazine* sometimes used the phrase well into the early 1900s,[15] and in 1898, at the Eighth Annual Meeting and Reunion of the United Confederate Veterans (the forerunner of today's Sons of Confederate Veterans), the following resolution was proposed: that from then on the Great War of 1861 was to be designated "the Civil War Between the States."[16]

CLARIFICATION

☛ To assist the reader in keeping track of the often confusing two-party political system referenced by early Americans writers and speakers before, during, and after Lincoln's War, I have inserted brackets identifying Victorian party affiliations where I deem appropriate.

PRESENTISM

☛ As a historian I view *presentism* (judging the past according to present day mores and customs) as the enemy of authentic history. And this is precisely why the Left employs it in its ongoing war against traditional American, conservative, and Christian values. By looking at history through the lens of modern day beliefs, they are able to distort, revise, and reshape the past into a false narrative that fits their ideological agenda: the liberalization *and* Northernization of America, the strengthening and further centralization of the national government, and total control of American political, economic, and social power, the same agenda that Lincoln championed.

This book, *The Unholy Crusade: Lincoln's Legacy of Destruction in the American South*, rejects presentism and replaces it with what I call *historicalism*: judging our ancestors based on the values of their own time. To get the most from this work the reader is invited to reject presentism as well. In this way—along with casting aside preconceived notions and the erroneous "history" churned out by our left-wing educational system—the truth in this work will be most readily ascertained and absorbed.

VIRGINIA FOCUS
☛ I have included more images of the ruins of Richmond, Virginia, than any other Southern city. Why? These were the most readily available, the easiest explanation probably being that its location made it the most accessible to photographers, particularly Northern photographers. However, there is another more obvious reason: Richmond was the capital of the Confederacy, making it both the ideal strategic and psychological target for the Liberals' hatred of the conservative South and her freedom-loving people.

STATES INCLUDED
☛ Most of the Southern states are missing from this book, such as North Carolina, Florida, and Texas. Why? Either there were no photos taken of the destruction in these states, or they have been lost, or, more likely,

suppressed. Thus in no way should this photographic compendium of Liberal violence be considered complete, or even partially complete.

It would be more correct to see my work as a mere introductory study of Liberal Lincoln's legacy of violence in the American South—with 99.99 percent of the photographic evidence in fact completely missing from the historical record. The photos herein, in other words, represent only the tiniest fraction of the havoc and devastation fomented on the conservative South by the North and its Liberal government, Liberal military, and Liberal populace. They are enough, however, to give the reader a realistic glimpse of what took place in the other Southern states.

CONFEDERATE DESTRUCTION
☛ Not all of the damage seen in the following images was caused by the North. The South sometimes found it expedient, for example, to burn

down a Confederate warehouse stocked with grain, weapons, or ammunition to prevent its contents from falling into the hands of the enemy. On other occasions Confederate militia were forced to blow up their own bridges to cut off pursuing Yanks. Such cases were few and far between, however; and in any event, responsibility for such damage must still be laid at the feet of Lincoln. For without his illegal invasion such wasteful and costly destruction would have been unnecessary.

VICTORIAN PHOTOGRAPHERS
☛ Concerning the 19th-Century photographers who took the photos used in this book: most are not known by name and are thus anonymous. Some who are known include: Alexander Gardner, Samuel A. Cooley, George N. Barnard, John Reekie, Andrew J. Russell, George Stacy, C. O. Bostwick, George S. Cook, G. O. Brown, James F. Gibson, and Timothy H. O'Sullivan. I am grateful to these men, to the Library of Congress, and to the many Victorian authors and publishers who  furnished images for *The Unholy Crusade*. Their diligent work is helping to preserve authentic American history into the 21st Century and beyond, particularly authentic *Southern* history.

CAPTIONS
☛ The caption with each photo or drawing contains the most accurate information I could procure regarding identity, location, etc. The known or probable date the image was produced is listed at the end of each caption. Photos of some locations appear more than once from different angles, by different photographers, at different times.

LEARN MORE
☛ Lincoln's War on the American people and the Constitution can never be fully understood without a thorough knowledge of the South's perspective. As this book is only meant to be a brief introductory guide to these topics, one cannot hope to learn the complete story here. For those who are interested in additional material from the South's perspective, please see my comprehensive histories listed on page 2.

Keep Your Body, Mind, & Spirit Vibrating at Their Highest Level

YOU CAN DO SO BY READING THE BOOKS OF

SEA RAVEN PRESS

There is nothing that will so perfectly keep your body, mind, and spirit in a healthy condition as to think wisely and positively. Hence you should not only read this book, but also the other books that we offer. They will quicken your physical, mental, and spiritual vibrations, enabling you to maintain a position in society as a healthy erudite person.

KEEP YOURSELF WELL-INFORMED!

The well-informed person is always at the head of the procession, while the ignorant, the lazy, and the unthoughtful hang onto the rear. If you are a Spiritual man or woman, do yourself a great favor: read Sea Raven Press books and stay well posted on the Truth. It is almost criminal for one to remain in ignorance while the opportunity to gain knowledge is open to all at a nominal price.

We invite you to visit our Webstore for a wide selection of wholesome, family-friendly, well-researched, educational books for all ages. You will be glad you did!

Five-Star Books & Gifts From the Heart of the American South

SeaRavenPress.com

INTRODUCTION

T he American Civil War (1861-1865) cost $20 billion—or about $4 million a day by 1865[17]—and, counting the second half of the conflict (so-called "Reconstruction," 1865-1877), lasted 16 horrific years. In the process hundreds of thousands of private homes and businesses were destroyed in the South, most which have disappeared without a trace: no court record or photograph to prove their existence, no monument to honor their long dead inhabitants, not even a wooden stake in the ground to mark the structures' original locations. All for what purpose?

Even more bizarre was the North's heartless plundering, torching, and utter ruination of the South's schools, universities, libraries, laboratories, churches, courthouses, hospitals, and even convents. In many cases Southern corpses were dug up, ransacked for valuables, and the entire cemetery was then blown to smithereens.[18] What drove Abraham Lincoln and his minions to such irrational violence?

It seems that nothing was sacred to the Yankee Liberals who invaded the conservative South. Though many behaved civilly and acted according to the law, a large percentage of Union officers and their

soldiers assumed the role of terrorists, smashing, pillaging, raping, murdering, burning, shooting, and bombing their way across Dixie. Between November 15 and December 21, 1864, Yankee General William T. Sherman alone cut a 60 mile swath several hundred miles long through Georgia, obliterating everything in his path. Beloved family pets, mainly dogs and cats, were shot on the spot, along with any other type of animal, such as horses, pigs, hogs, geese, and cattle, that could not be carried off. In one typical case a Union soldier saw some Southern children playing with a frisky young greyhound. Walking over to the startled youngsters, the insolent bluecoat grabbed the puppy and cruelly pummeled its brains out in front of them.[19]

A Southern history book from 1920 describes Sherman's march like this:

The redoubtable William Tecumseh Sherman, "the Union Butcher from Ohio."

Sherman burned Atlanta and with sixty-two thousand men started on his famous march to the sea. "I propose to sally forth to ruin Georgia," he said. In a region sixty miles wide from Atlanta to Savannah all foodstuff was destroyed and the cattle and horses driven off. Sherman justified his policy upon the theory that it was the quickest way to end the war. There was practically no resistance to this vast confiscating horde, and by December the Federal army reached Savannah. Sherman's message to President Lincoln was: "I beg to present, as a Christmas gift, the city of Savannah with one hundred and fifty heavy guns, plenty of ammunition, also about twenty-five thousand bales of cotton."

Sherman moved northward into South Carolina in February, 1865. The Federal army seemed filled with the desire to wreak vengeance on the state that had first withdrawn from the Union, and ruin marked every foot of the advance. Columbia surrendered to the enemy and was burned. Charleston and then Wilmington were occupied by the invader. On March 20, 1865, Sherman was at Goldsboro, North Carolina, and Grant was at Petersburg, just one hundred and fifty miles away. So far Sherman had met with little resistance; the principal difficulty in his march had been the winter rains and swollen rivers and swamps.[20]

Those Atlantans who were not beaten, arrested, or killed by Sherman, fled into the mountains. Those civilians unlucky enough to be left behind faced a demonic force of unparalleled evil. Writes Stonebraker:

At one place Sherman took four hundred factory girls and sent them north of the Ohio River, away from home and friends. Such things are inhuman, and one's blood is made to boil to even relate them.

All the white inhabitants were made to leave the city without regard to age or condition. All who would not take Lincoln's oath [of allegiance to the Union] were sent South to famish. Such a stream of men, women and children with their all in their hands, could be seen wending their way from the desolated city. [Confederate General John Bell] Hood retorted against this cruelty, but Sherman said, "War is cruelty! This year we will take your property, and next year your lives!"[21]

In their wake Union troops often left nothing but thousands of solitary charred chimney stacks, known as "Sherman's sentinels," and miles of grotesquely twisted railroad track, known as "Sherman's neckties," to indicate their wicked progress. Steel-toed boots aided Yankee thugs in their destruction, enabling them to kick down the strongest doors and break open the toughest locks.[22]

"Sherman's sentinels."

Following in Sherman's path were the bummers: great mobs of criminals, felons, outlaws, refugees, prostitutes, and stevedores, picking through the spoils of devastation, preying on the Southern victims of the general's wrath.[23] Finally, rounding up this motley menagerie, were trailing throngs of newly freed black servants, homeless, hungry, and confused. Southern whites, surely the best friend the black man has ever had,[24] could not help them now, and Sherman, a lifelong racist, was certainly not going to.[25]

According to Sherman himself, there was only one way to subdue an "immoral population" like Dixie, and that was by using a scorched-earth policy of total war.[26] Said the impudent Ohioan:

I would banish all minor questions, assert the broad doctrine that as a nation the United States has the right, and also the physical power, to penetrate to every part of our national domain, and that we will do it—that we will do it in our own time and in our own way; that it makes no difference whether it be in one year, or two, or ten, or twenty; that we will remove and destroy every obstacle, if need be, take every life, every acre of land, every particle of property, everything that to us seems proper; that we will not cease till the end is attained; that all who do not aid us are enemies, and that we will not account to them for our acts. If the people of the South oppose, they do so at their peril; and if they stand by, mere lookers-on in this domestic tragedy, they have no right to immunity, protection, or share in the final results.

. . . In accepting war, it should be "pure and simple" as applied to the belligerents. I would keep it so, till all traces of the war are effaced; till those who appealed to it are sick and tired of it, and come to the emblem of our nation, and sue for peace. I would not coax them, or even meet them half-way, but make them so sick of war that generations would pass away before they would again appeal to it.[27]

Again, when Sherman ordered all of the residents of Atlanta to evacuate the city, Confederate General Hood, commander of the Army of Tennessee, beseeched him "in the name of God and humanity" to allow them to remain, for "you are expelling from their homes and firesides the wives and children of a brave people."[28] Sherman's reply was icy and predictable:

If the people raise a howl against my barbarity and cruelty, I will answer that war is war, and not popularity-seeking. If they want peace, they and their relatives must stop the war.[29]

Confederate General John Bell Hood.

It would be difficult to find a more hateful, arrogant, and ignorant Yankee attitude toward the South.

Though only military resources were supposed to have been destroyed, Sherman and his henchmen also went after private homes and businesses, gutting, in fact, most of the town.[30] After more than a month of bombardment, the once magnificent city was turned to pebbles.[31] Some 1,600 people (mostly seniors, women, and children) were evicted from their Atlanta homes before Sherman was through.[32] Here was inhumanity at its peak.

At Roswell, Georgia, General Sherman, Lincoln's most ruthless henchman—deemed "unstable and mentally deranged" even by other Yankees[33]—ordered his men to destroy every mill and factory in the area, arrest the employees (male and female) on charge of "treason," then murder the innocent owners.[34] In another order he demanded of his troops that their "destruction be so thorough that not a rail or tie can be used again,"[35] then boasted that many of the towns he and his army marched through would not be found on future maps.[36] On March 7, 1864, he reported on one of these, Meridian, Mississippi, saying:

Confederate General Nathan Bedford Forrest.

> For five days 10,000 men worked hard and with a will in that work of destruction, with axes, crowbars, sledges, clawbars, and with fire, and I have no hesitation in pronouncing the work as well done. Meridian, with its depots, store-houses, arsenal, hospitals, offices, hotels, and cantonments, no longer exists.[37]

I repeat here Sherman's arrogant pronouncement: "Meridian no longer exists."

The town was later rebuilt. But to this day the only evidence that many of the places he obliterated were once thriving communities are small stone markers.[38]

After literally wiping the city of Meridian, Mississippi, off the map,[39] no city or form of destruction was off limits. It was at this time that Sherman made official his policy of waging war on noncombatants, an obvious admission that the North was losing and that Yankee armies could not win on the battlefield against "bold and enterprising" Confederate officers like Nathan Bedford Forrest.[40]

From then on, Sherman robbed, burned, and blasted his way through the rest of the Magnolia State, cutting, as he bragged, "a swath of desolation fifty miles broad across the state of Mississippi, which the present generation will not forget."[41] In Savannah, Georgia, he crowed that 80 percent of the devastation he had caused was "simple waste and destruction."[42] In late 1864, as noted above, after subduing and occupying the city, a cocky Sherman sent a telegram to Lincoln, offering the defeated town to him as a Christmas present.[43] Here is the president's reply:

> My Dear General Sherman,—Many, many thanks for your Christmas gift,—the capture of Savannah. When you were about to leave Atlanta for the Atlantic, I was anxious, if not fearful; but feeling that you were the better judge, and remembering that "nothing risked, nothing gained," I did not interfere. Now, this undertaking being a success, the honor is all yours; for I believe that none of us went further than to acquiesce. And taking the work of [Union] General [George H.] Thomas into the count, as it should be taken, it is indeed a great success. Not only does it afford the obvious and immediate military advantages, but in showing to the world that your army could be divided, putting the stronger part to an important new service, and yet leaving enough to vanquish the old opposing forces of the whole,—Hood's army,—it brings those who sat in darkness to see a great light.
>
> But what next? I suppose it will be safe, if I leave General Grant and yourself to decide. Please make my grateful acknowledgments to your whole army,—officers and men. Yours very truly, A. Lincoln.[44]

Union President Abraham Lincoln.

If nothing else, Lincoln's enthusiastic response reveals his complicity in Sherman's war crimes—but there is more.

Not only had he personally issued military orders that violated the Geneva Convention, but he also personally approved his officers' illegalities, such as Sherman's plan to level Georgia to the ground, as well as the red-head's total war and scorched earth policies. After all, General Robert E. Lee took his orders directly from Confederate President Jefferson Davis. It is obvious then that Sherman, Grant, Sheridan, and the rest took their orders directly from Lincoln.[45]

Why else would "Honest Abe" repeatedly dine with, thank, reward, and promote men like Grant and Sherman? Indeed, not only had Lincoln been in constant telegraph contact with both officers throughout the War, but on March 28, 1865, he excitedly met with them at City Point, Virginia, to hear about their "achievements" and congratulate them on their work in person.[46] Only a few months earlier he had sent a telegram to Grant in the field that read:

Hold on with a bulldog grip, and chew and choke as much as possible.[47]

What Lincoln meant by these words would have been clear to every Southerner. They were certainly well understood by Grant, for he acted on them to the letter.

Like Lincoln, Sherman held special loathing for South Carolina: it was the first Southern state to secede and the home of numerous and fiercely anti-North fire-eaters. As he approached the Palmetto State, Sherman's army was "burning with an insatiable desire to wreak vengeance" on it, a sentiment with which the Yankee officer concurred, ominously promising: "I almost tremble at her fate, but feel that she deserves all that is in store for her."[48]

Union General Ulysses S. Grant.

South Carolina's "fate" under Sherman's auspices was later described by Reverend Dr. John Bachman of Charleston:

When Sherman's army came sweeping through Carolina, leaving a broad track of desolation for hundreds of miles, whose steps were accompanied with fire, and sword, and blood . . . I happened to be at Cash's Depot, six miles from Cheraw. The owner was a widow, Mrs. Ellerbe, seventy-one years of age. Her son, Colonel Cash, was absent. I witnessed the barbarities inflicted on the aged, the widow, and young and delicate females. [Yankee officers,] high in command, were engaged tearing from the ladies their watches, their ear and wedding rings, the daguerreotypes [a type of early photograph] of those they loved and cherished. A lady of delicacy and refinement, a personal friend, was compelled to strip before them, that they might find concealed watches and other valuables under her dress.

A system of torture was practiced toward the weak, unarmed, and defenseless, which as far as I know and believe, was universal throughout the whole course of that invading army. Before they arrived at a plantation, they inquired the names of the most faithful and trustworthy family servants; these

were immediately seized, pistols were presented at their heads; with the most terrific curses, they were threatened to be shot if they did not assist them in finding buried treasures. If this did not succeed, they were tied up and cruelly beaten. Several poor creatures died under the infliction. The last resort was that of hanging, and the officers and men of the triumphant army of General Sherman were engaged in erecting gallows and hanging up these faithful and devoted [black] servants. They were strung up until life was nearly extinct, when they were let down, suffered to rest awhile, then threatened and hung up again. It is not surprising that some should have been left hanging so long that they were taken down dead.

Coolly and deliberately these hardened men proceeded on their way, as if they had perpetrated no crime, and as if the God of heaven would not pursue them with his vengeance. But it was not alone the poor blacks to whom they professed to come as liberators that were thus subjected to torture and death. Gentlemen of high character, pure and honorable and gray-headed, unconnected with the military, were dragged from their fields or their beds, and subjected to this process of threats, beating, and hanging. Along the whole track of Sherman's army, traces remain of the cruelty and inhumanity practiced on the aged and the defenseless. Some of those who were hung up died under the rope, while their cruel murderers have not only been left unreproached and unhung, but have been hailed as heroes and patriots [by other Yankee Liberals]. The list of those martyrs whom the cupidity of the officers and men of Sherman's army sacrificed to their thirst for gold and silver, is large and most revolting.[49]

Not even the religious were spared. On March 5, 1865, famed South Carolina belle Mary Chesnut recorded the following in her diary:

Sherman's men had burned the convent. . . . Men were rolling tar barrels and lighting torches to fling on the house when the nuns came. Columbia is but dust and ashes, burned to the ground. Men, women, and children are left there, houseless, homeless, without a particle of food—reduced to picking up corn that was left by Sherman's horses on picket grounds and parching it to stay their hunger.[50]

Many fellow Northerners were horrified by Sherman's actions. One of them happened to be a Yankee officer, General Don Carlos Buell. After resigning from the military over the issue, he said:

> I believe that the policy and means with which the war was being prosecuted [by the Union] were discreditable to the nation and a stain upon civilization.[51]

Another Yankee General, diehard anti-American socialist and Lincoln devotee Carl Schurz—no friend of the traditional South—also journeyed through Dixie in 1865, and recorded this observation:

> My travels in the interior took me to the track of Sherman's march, which, in South Carolina at least, looked for many miles like a broad black streak of ruin and desolation—the fences all gone; lonesome smoke stacks, surrounded by dark heaps of ashes and cinders, marking the spots where human habitations had stood; the fields along the road wildly overgrown by weeds, with here and there a sickly looking patch of cotton or corn cultivated by negro squatters. In the city of Columbia, the political capital of the State, I found a thin fringe of houses encircling a confused mass of charred ruins of dwellings and business buildings, which had been destroyed by a sweeping conflagration.[52]

In all, Sherman's "March to the Sea" inflicted some $100 million of damage on Georgia alone, almost $2.25 billion in today's currency. It was for this remorseless devastation that Henry C. Work's ode to Sherman, "Marching Through Georgia," became the most detested song in Dixie, and Sherman himself became the most hated man across the South—for a time even more so than Lincoln.[53]

Union General and South-hating socialist Carl Schurz.

Sherman rubbed salt into the wound he had created by joking that he would "bring every wealthy white Southern woman to the washtub."[54] The insult did not go unnoticed by the Carolina aristocracy, further inflaming South-North animosities.[55]

During his "March to the Sea," Sherman, by his own admission, not

Union General Louis Douglass Watkins.

only caused irreparable damage to the South's infrastructure, but he also inflicted his devastating violence on her innocent and terrified civilian population—all with the full knowledge, approval, and encouragement of Lincoln. Private residences, barns, servants' quarters, mansions, granaries, plantations, ginhouses, even places of worship, were looted then burned to the ground, along with countless other "pointless acts of vandalism and destruction."[56]

And Sherman had the temerity to call Confederate General Nathan Bedford Forrest the "Devil"![57]

For those who still doubt the North's innate criminality as well as its destructive and sanguinary intentions toward Dixie, below I offer just two examples of Sherman's many official field dispatches. As he so often did, he calls not only for the demolition of non-military property, but also for the murder of unarmed Southern civilians:

> Hdqrs. Military Division of the Mississippi, in the field, Rome, Ga., October 29, 1864. Brigadier-General [Louis Douglass] Watkins, Calhoun, Ga.:
> Cannot you send over about Fairmount and Adairsville, burn ten or twelve houses of known secessionists, kill a few at random, and let them know that it will be repeated every time a train is fired on from Resaca to Kingston? W. T. Sherman, Major-General, Commanding.[58]

In November 1864 Sherman ordered the burning of the town of Columbus, Kentucky, rather than let it fall into Confederate hands. His official report reads:

> Hdqrs. Military Division of the Mississippi, in the field, Kingston, Ga., November 5, 1864. Col. J. N. McArthur, Commanding Post, Columbus, Ky.:
> Dispatch received. Eight hundred men are plenty. When I refer to Columbus I refer to the forts and guns, not the town. I don't care a cent about the town. If the enemy approaches Columbus the guns of large caliber must be defended to the death and the town should be burned by you rather

than that Forrest should get a pound of provisions or forage. Any attack on Columbus will be a mere dash, and Forrest will not attack men, no matter what their number, who show a determination to fight. W. T. Sherman, Major-General.[59]

Sherman's violent loathing of the South has been returned to him a thousand times over by traditional Southerners who, to this day, 150 years on, wince in disgust at the very mention of his name.[60]

But "Uncle Billy," as his fawning soldiers called him, was far from the only Yankee officer who relished bullying, terrorizing, and effacing the South. Many hundreds of other devilish senior U.S. officials could be named, among them Union Generals Benjamin F. "The Beast" Butler, Edward Hatch, David Hunter, Edward Moody McCook, Robert Huston Milroy, John McCauley Palmer, John Pope, Philip Henry Sheridan, Andrew Jackson Smith, William Sooy Smith, and James Harrison Wilson. I do not list these men's names casually. At one time or another, all were occupied in nefarious activities in the South, ranging from minor cruelties to extreme and unnecessary violence, breaking most of the accepted rules of warfare and international law along the way.

One Union officer who is still held in particular contempt here in the South is General John Thomas Croxton, the man responsible for burning down the University of Alabama.[61] Another dastardly individual who must be mentioned is Union Colonel Fielding Hurst, who was known to engage in extortion, theft, torture, mutilation, and

Union General John Thomas Croxton.

the murder of numerous innocent Southern civilians, including the "wanton shooting" of a "deformed and helpless" 16 year old Tennessee boy.[62] Examples of humane, moral, law-abiding Yankee officers do exist, of course, such as General Godfrey Weitzel, whom I am happy to mention.[63] But unfortunately their memories are lost amid the overwhelming chronicles of Yankee maliciousness and lawlessness.

Confederate General Jubal Anderson Early followed Yankee General David Hunter through the Shenandoah Valley, the "Breadbasket of the

Confederacy," and so became just one of millions of eyewitnesses to the many war crimes perpetuated under the auspices of President Lincoln.

In his book, *A Memoir of the Last Year of the War for Independence in the Confederate States of America*, Early describes what he saw:

Confederate General Jubal Anderson Early.

The scenes on Hunter's route from Lynchburg [Virginia] had been truly heart-rending. Houses had been burned, and helpless women and children left without shelter. The country had been stripped of provisions and many families left without a morsel to eat. Furniture and bedding had been cut to pieces, and old men and women and children robbed of all the clothing they had except that on their backs. Ladies trunks had been rifled and their dresses torn to pieces in mere wantonness. Even the negro girls had lost their little finery.

We now had renewed evidences of the outrages committed by Hunter's orders in burning and plundering private houses. We saw the ruins of a number of houses to which the torch had been applied by his orders. At Lexington he had burned the Military Institute, with all of its contents, including its library and scientific apparatus; and Washington College had been plundered and the statue of Washington stolen. The residence of Ex-Governor [John] Letcher at that place had been burned by orders, and but a few minutes given Mrs. Letcher and her family to leave the house. In the same county a most excellent Christian gentlemen, a Mr. Creigh, had been hung, because, on a former occasion he had killed a straggling and marauding Federal soldier while in the act of insulting and outraging the ladies of his family.

These are but some of the outrages committed by Hunter or his orders, and I will not insult the memory of the ancient barbarians of the North by calling them "acts of Vandalism." If those old barbarians were savage and cruel, they at least had the manliness and daring of rude soldiers, with occasional traits of magnanimity. Hunter's deeds were those of a malignant and cowardly fanatic, who was better qualified to make war upon helpless women and children than upon armed soldiers.[64]

Yankee war criminal General Philip Henry Sheridan was no less barbaric and unfeeling. During the Union's Shenandoah Valley Campaign, he personally approved the torching of barns and crops, after which he and his men left the region a blackened wasteland, pillaging, firing, and murdering as they went. Sheridan then joked that "a crow could not fly over it without carrying his rations with him." Civilians who opposed him were hanged on the spot. In October 1864, he boasted to Grant:

> I have destroyed over 2,000 barns, filled with wheat, hay, and farming implements; over 70 mills, filled with flour and wheat; have driven in front of the army over 4,000 head of stock, and have killed and issued to the troops not less than 3,000 sheep. . . . all the houses within an area of five miles were burned.[65]

Sheridan's soldiers bragged that "we stripped the Valley to the bare earth; when we got through there weren't enough crumbs left to feed a pigeon." Sheridan himself—a man who, for "some light entertainment," would often burn every fifth house—pronounced his "scorched earth" approach to warfare a "humanitarian" policy, since he believed that Southerners would submit to Lincolnian liberalism rather than die of starvation.[66] He was wrong!

Union General Philip Henry Sheridan.

A Confederate officer who survived the Shenandoah Holocaust described the scene this way:

> I rode down the Valley with the advance after Sheridan's retreating cavalry beneath great columns of smoke which almost shut out the sun by day, and in the red glare of bonfires which, all across the Valley, poured out flames and sparks heavenward and crackled mockingly in the night air; and I saw mothers and maidens tearing their hair and shrieking to Heaven in their fright and despair, and little children, voiceless and tearless in their pitiable terror.[67]

Union General Ulysses S. Grant, who was soon to become America's second worst president, was no better than Sheridan or Sherman. In several letters to Sheridan, dated August 16, 1864, he ordered the needless destruction of private property (adding theft to the crime), the murder of Rebel soldiers "without trial," and the hostage taking, military arrest, and imprisonment of noncombatants (civilians), all illegal. One of these shocking dispatches has been preserved in the ORA. Grant writes:

> The families of most of [Confederate Colonel John S.] Mosby's men are known, and can be collected. I think they should be taken and kept at Fort McHenry or some secure place, as hostages for the good conduct of Mosby and his men. Where any of Mosby's men are caught hang them without trial. . . . If you can possibly spare a division of cavalry, send them through Loudoun County [Virginia], to destroy and carry off the crops, animals, negroes, and all men under fifty years of age capable of bearing arms. In this way you will get many of Mosby's men. All male citizens under fifty can fairly be held as prisoners of war, and not as citizen prisoners.[68]

Just weeks before, on August 5, 1864, Grant had written to General Hunter:

Union General David Hunter.

> In pushing up the Shenandoah Valley, where it is expected you will have to go first or last, it is desirable that nothing should be left to invite the enemy to return. Take all provisions, forage, and stock wanted for the use of your command; such as cannot be consumed destroy.[69]

One of those closest to Lincoln was his chief of staff at the time, Union General Henry Wager Halleck, a man who proved himself to be very knowledgeable in the various methods of ruining soil and destroying cities. It was Halleck who, in daily contact with the president, wrote the following to Sherman on December 18, 1864:

> Should you capture Charleston, I hope that by some accident the place may be destroyed, and if a little salt should be sown upon its site it may prevent the growth of future crops of nullification and secession.[70]

The memo was from Halleck. But the "message" was from Lincoln.

In an official report dated March 25, 1862, Halleck made the following confession from his headquarters at St. Louis, Missouri, to Lincoln's Secretary of War Edwin McMasters Stanton:

> It cannot be denied that some of our volunteer regiments have behaved very badly, plundering to an enormous extent. I have done everything in my power to prevent this and to punish the guilty. Many of the regimental officers are very bad men and participate in this plunder.[71]

Union General Henry Wager Hallack.

European-Americans were not the only ones to suffer under the Yankee's illicit and bloody invasion. African-Americans, the very people Lincoln's troops were allegedly invading the South to "liberate," were particularly targeted by white Union soldiers. The following field dispatch (dated December 30, 1864) from Union General Rufus Saxton to Stanton, offers a glimpse into the violent, sordid, crime-infested thugocracy created by "mob boss" Lincoln. Reporting from his post at Beaufort, South Carolina, the appalled Yankee Saxton writes:

> I found the prejudice of color and race here [in this U.S. camp] in full force, and the general feeling of the army of occupation was unfriendly to the blacks. It was manifested in various forms of personal insult and abuse, in depredations on their plantations, stealing and destroying their crops and domestic animals, and robbing them of their money.
>
> The [Negro] women were held as the legitimate prey of lust, and as they had been taught it was a crime to resist a white man they had not learned to dare to defend their chastity. Licentiousness was widespread . . . in the [Northern] army of occupation. Among our [Union] officers and soldiers there were many honorable exceptions to this, but the influence of too many was demoralizing to the negro, and has greatly hindered the efforts for their improvement and elevation. There was a general disposition among the [U.S.] soldiers and civilian speculators here to defraud the negroes in their private traffic, to take the commodities which they offered for sale by force, or to pay for them in worthless money.
>
> At one time these practices were so frequent and notorious that the

negroes would not bring their produce to market for fear of being plundered. Other occurrences have tended to cool the enthusiastic joy with which the coming of the Yankees was welcomed.[72]

Union General Rufus Saxton.

As we have seen, other forms of Yankee criminality included the raiding of grand Southern estates, in which families were insulted and assaulted, their valuables broken up or torn to pieces: paintings, heirlooms, pianos, dishware, cabinetry, and furniture, all turned to kindling and set on fire as the occupants fled for their lives. No age, race, or gender was spared. Both girls and elderly women had their jewelry ripped from their fingers, ears, wrists, and necks at gunpoint, while boys and men were forced to hand over their watches as Union soldiers looked on, laughing sardonically.[73]

In 1868 Southern writers Thomas Jordan and John P. Pryor described some of the military practices of Union war criminal William Sooy Smith in Mississippi:

The Federal advance . . . did not enter Oxford until about eight o'clock on the morning of the 22nd, but a column of [U.S.] infantry soon followed. The cavalry were speedily and widely scattered through the town, but the infantry were kept in ranks. Up to noon, although there were a number of petty acts of spoliation on the part of individual soldiers, yet no general disposition was shown either to license or commit arson and rapine. The railroad depot was burned in the morning, but, as yet, no private buildings were set on fire. Suddenly, about midday, however, this forbearance ceased. Orders were then given by the Federal commander for the burning of the public buildings and unoccupied houses; and in a little while, to quote the language of a Federal chronicler,

"the public square was surrounded by a canopy of flame; the splendid courthouse was among the buildings destroyed, with other edifices of a public character. In fact, where once stood a handsome little country town, now only remained the blackened skeletons of the houses, and the smouldering ruins that marked the track of war."

In this conflagration were consumed all the principal business houses, with one accidental exception, the two brick hotels of the place, and, of course, the flames speedily spread to several dwellings occupied by women and children, and sick persons happily rescued, however, from destruction by the exertions of the inhabitants of Oxford.

One occupied mansion, howbeit, was burned to the ground under circumstances which make the act noteworthy in these pages. . . . Mrs. Thompson's house, several days previously, had been despoiled by the Federal cavalry commander and his men. Major-General Smith now sent an officer of his staff with a detachment to burn it. Mrs. Thompson made a dignified, earnest, but vain appeal that her house might be spared her. Only fifteen minutes were granted for the removal of any articles which she might specially wish to save; but these, as fast as they were brought from the house, in the presence of Federal officers, were ruthlessly stolen from her by the soldiery who clustered around, so that scarcely an article, other than the clothing on her person, escaped fire or pillage.

Up to midday, guards had been set as if to repress pillage; these were withdrawn about that time, and for several hours thereafter Oxford was delivered up to riot and rapacity. Houses on all sides were broken into and despoiled of clothing, bedding, and provisions, which, if not carried off, were maliciously destroyed.

Carpets were torn up, curtains cut down, and furniture broken in downright wantonness; and in a number of instances the torch was set to houses thus rifled, and only the exertions of their terrified occupants saved them from destruction. Some subaltern [Union] officers were greatly chagrined, and displayed a disposition to restrain their men from acts so disgraceful to their vaunted flag; but no officer of rank was heard to interpose his authority for the suppression of disorder in a place which there had been no effort to defend, nor any conflict in its immediate vicinity. The men, thus assured of the countenance of their commander, set all opposition to their licentiousness at defiance, until five P.M., when they were suddenly withdrawn, and the enemy began their retreat northward so rapidly as to reach Holly Springs by ten A.M., on the next day.

Union General William Sooy Smith.

So completely, however, had they done their work in Oxford, that its non-combatant inhabitants, mostly women and children, were left absolutely destitute of food until the soldiers' rough rations could be brought up from the Confederate depots south of the Yocona [River], and distributed among them.[74]

Union Secretary of War Edwin McMasters Stanton.

The looting and burning of homes, along with the torturing and killing of captured prisoners of war is, of course, illegal and immoral, as is torturing and killing noncombatants and civilians. But military and religious law did not prevent Union forces from engaging in both of these monstrous practices.[75]

Like their white counterparts, African-American women were sometimes beaten and raped,[76] while African-American men of eligible age were rounded up and forced to enlist in the Union army at the tip of a bayonet.[77] Those who refused were often shot on the spot. The young, the feeble, the aged, and females were sent off to so-called "government plantations," Southern farms whose peaceful and harmless white owners had been driven off or killed.[78] Here so-called "freed" black men, women, and children were put to work doing ordinary labor, the same drudgery they had performed previously as slaves (mainly laundry, cooking, and cleaning), and from which the Union was purportedly trying to free them. A ten-hour work day, twenty-six days a month, was mandatory. The pay was $10 a month ($0.26 a day, or 2.6 cents an hour). "Insubordination" was punishable by "imprisonment in darkness on bread and water." This was Lincoln's idea of "emancipation."[79]

When it was all over, much of the South lay in ruins, little more than smouldering rubble, with millions of homeless men, women, and children now refugees in their own country. "Reconstruction" was merely another 12 years of vengeance and war on Dixie, with Yankee soldiers stationed on every street corner, where they harassed and often illegally arrested and tortured harmless civilians who were doing nothing more than trying to rebuild their lives after the previous four years of Yankee death and destruction.[80]

Northern Liberals intentionally turned Southern life upside down. Illiterate blacks were given important political seats while highly educated former Confederate soldiers were prohibited from holding office.[81] They were also banned from wearing their Confederate uniforms,[82] or risk arrest and imprisonment, usually without the writ of *habeas corpus*—another one of the North's many unconstitutional war crimes.[83] In violation of the First Amendment even the sale of Confederate flags was now illegal in the South.[84]

Intelligent people want to know why. What was the purpose of degrading, humiliating, and punishing the Southern people for 16 long years? Why destroy their homes, tear down their stores, burn their crops, level their schools and libraries, and even kill family pets? What kind of inhumanity prompted the demolishing of Southern cemeteries, hospitals, and churches? What was the motivation for all of the bloodshed, devastation, and mayhem? What incited millions of Northerners to take up arms against their fellow Americans, ruthlessly torching, shooting, and bombing their way across the South for almost 20 years?

Educated intellectually curious people no longer believe that Lincoln drained the U.S. Treasury, wasted hundreds of thousands of lives, and called for war on the South against the wishes of the majority of Americans and even his own cabinet, in order to either "preserve the Union" or "abolish slavery." Neither do they any longer accept the opposite fiction; namely that the South fought in order to "destroy the Union" or "preserve slavery." In this

Union soldiers enter a Southern mansion and violently confront the lady of the house. After she and her family were thrown into the street, her beautiful home was pillaged and torched, all violations of moral and civil law.

day and age what sane person could possibly accept any of these obvious Yankee myths, purposefully invented to mislead, disguise, and confuse?

Why then the massive Northern campaign of death and destruction against Dixieland? It was all due to the Liberal's age-old *hatred* of the Conservative, traditional, Christian South, his craven lust for full political *power*, and his insatiable desire for absolute *control* of the American people, their income, their property, their education, their healthcare, their food, their housing, their religion, and their guns.

In 1896 William McKinley became the first Conservative presidential candidate selected by the Republican Party. Up until that year it had been the party of progressives, dating back to its founding by Liberals and Socialists in 1854. This means that Abraham Lincoln, though a Republican in 1860 and 1864, was a Liberal.

It is a little known fact today, even to many Southerners and Conservatives, that *the Republicans of the Civil War era were Liberals while the Democrats of the Civil War era were Conservatives*. The Republican Party was founded in 1854 by a group of Liberals and Socialists who disliked the U.S. Constitution and states' rights, and believed that the U.S. would be better off as an "indivisible nation" built on socialistic big government principles.[85]

Democrats, the Conservative Party in the 1860s, held the opposite view, that the Founding Fathers purposefully created the U.S. and her Constitution around conservative principles, and that this tradition should not be tampered with.[86]

Thus there were two violently opposing theories of government in 1860: a Liberal one and a Conservative one.

Just as is the case today, most Victorian Liberals lived in the Northern states, and most Victorian Conservatives lived in the Southern states. And here we have the seeds of the American Civil War, often incorrectly called the "War between the States," "War between the North and South," the "War between the Blue and the Gray," the "War between the Union and the Confederacy." These labels, however, only serve to further muddle the issue concerning the cause of the War, which at its root was nothing more than a 16 year fight started by Northern Liberals for the purpose of crushing Southern Conservatism—one of the bloodiest and most useless conflicts waged in the history of the world.[87]

The Conservative South seceded legally, and in accordance with the Constitution (see the Ninth and Tenth Amendments, which tacitly allow both accession and secession).[88] The Confederacy had no designs whatsoever on the U.S. government, as South-haters preach. It only asked to be left alone,[89] and even offered to pay for any debts incurred due to its separation from the Union.[90]

The Liberal North, on the other hand, refused to recognize the right of secession (the same right by which the American colonies separated from England), and instead aggressively, illicitly, and unnecessarily sent 75,000 troops to invade and occupy the legally created sovereign republic named "The Confederate States of America" after the nickname for the original U.S.A.[91] The photographs, illustrations, and drawings which fill this book are the result of that invasion and occupation. After perusing them I am sure the reader will come away with the same conclusion that all astute people do after an honest and thorough study of the Southern view of Lincoln's War. As Samuel Augustus Steel

In 1896 William Jennings Bryan became the first Liberal presidential candidate selected by the Democratic Party. Up until that year it had been the party of Conservatives, dating back to its founding by traditional Constitutionalists and antifederalists in 1828. This means that Jefferson Davis, though a Democrat in 1860 and 1864, was a Conservative.

said in 1914, "the South was right,"[92] and this poignant pictorial work proves it.

When all is said and done, who was personally responsible for the demolition of the Old South and the degradation, inhumanity, anguish, brutality, torture, and murder of her people, and for the reckless disregard of international law, the U.S. Constitution, and the Geneva Conventions between April 12, 1861 and April 9, 1865? As my subtitle shows, it is all part of the legacy of big government Liberal Abraham Lincoln. Evidence comes from a thousand different sources, none more compelling than from Lincoln himself.

The official public stamp of approval for the commission of war crimes in the South came from the Liberal U.S. Congress acting under Lincoln's influence, which gave Grant, Sheridan, and Sherman the "Thanks of Congress" for achieving "significant victories" during the War (Sherman received two).[93] These "significant victories," of course, were often the result of scorched-earth, total war policies that included larceny, wide destruction of civilian property, rape, maiming, torture, and the mass murder of Southern noncombatants.[94]

Of the war crimes of Lincoln's commanders, the Honorable Judge George L. Christian of Virginia wrote in 1909:

> We know . . . that these officers would not have dared to thus violate [the rules of civilized warfare] . . . unless these violations had been known by them to be sanctioned by their official head, Mr. Lincoln, from whom they received their appointments and commissions, and whose duty it was to prevent such violations and outrages.
>
> . . . Who alone had any semblance of authority to give this permission to Sherman and who gave it? There can be but one answer—Abraham Lincoln, the then President of the United States. Will the people of the South lick the hand that thus smote their fathers, their mothers, their brethren and their sisters by now singing paeans of glory to his name and fame?
>
> . . . We charge, and without the fear of successful contradiction, that Mr. Lincoln, as the head of the Federal Government, and the Commander-in-Chief of its armies, was directly responsible for the outrages committed by his subordinates; and that the future and unprejudiced historian will so hold him responsible. We verily believe.
>
> But this is not all. Mr. Lincoln was [also] directly responsible for all the sorrows, sufferings and deaths of prisoners on both sides during the war.[95]

A complete compilation of "all the sorrows, sufferings, and deaths" committed by Lincoln and his men would fill volumes. The Yankee president was well aware of nearly all of them and directly, or more often indirectly (to legally protect himself), sanctioned them.[96]

If there is any doubt as to Lincoln's knowledge and involvement, consider the case of one of Lincoln's generals, John B. Turchin. Turchin was rightfully ousted from the Yankee army by his superiors for burning down the town of Athens,

ABRAHAM LINCOLN,
REPUBLICAN CANDIDATE FOR PRESIDENT OF THE UNITED STATES.

An 1860 Republican campaign poster promoting Liberal Lincoln as presidential nominee.

Alabama, in 1862. However, Lincoln later reversed the order, restored Turchin to his command, and even gave him a promotion.[97]

Confederate President Jefferson Davis, known in the South as the "Patriot of Patriots," and the most important Conservative in American history.

Why did big government Liberal Lincoln push his officers to win at any cost, even to the point of destroying entire cities and savagely murdering thousands of innocent Southern men, women, and children of all races? As mentioned, politics, of course. The upcoming 1864 election weighed heavily on Lincoln's mind throughout 1863 and early 1864. He felt that victories in the field would mean a victory at the polls. And he was correct. Sherman's and Sheridan's many successes during this period gave the president a 10 percent margin that November, all he needed to be reelected.[98]

What then was the end result of the ultimate war between Conservatism and Liberalism in 1861?

It was not abolition, because Davis and Lincoln repeatedly said the conflict did not concern slavery—as did both Confederate and Union soldiers.[99] Additionally, even *before* the conflict started Davis recognized that the "peculiar institution" was about to go extinct,[100] and began planning for South-wide emancipation as early as January 1865, four months *before* the War ended.[101] As further proof we have the fact that American slavery was not officially abolished until 8 months *after* the War terminated and Lincoln died, when the Thirteenth Amendment (offered by a Southerner, John Brooks Henderson of Missouri) was ratified in December 1865.[102]

The War was certainly not about "preserving the Union," for the original Union created by the Founding Fathers was a *voluntary* one.[103] Lincoln's War, however, destroyed it and replaced it with an *involuntary* one.[104] In turn, because of this, the South's effort to preserve the Founders' original Union and Constitution was itself unsuccessful.[105]

The true legacy of the conflict?

On July 20, 1861, only four months after the start of the conflict, our beloved Confederate President Jefferson Davis was already speaking out against Lincoln's accumulating war crimes, condemning America's sixteenth chief executive for destroying "private residences in peaceful rural retreats," and for the "outrages [rapes] committed on defenseless [Southern] females by [Yankee] soldiers."[106] In bringing nationwide attention to Lincoln's crimes, Davis made special note of the following:

> In this war, rapine is the rule; private houses, in beautiful rural retreats, are bombarded and burnt; grain crops in the field are consumed by the torch, and, when the torch is not convenient, careful labour is bestowed to render complete destruction of every article of use or ornament remaining in private dwellings, after their inhabitants have fled from the outrages of brute soldiery.[107]

Since those terrible years Dixie has fully rebuilt herself and is now once again a thriving region, with a booming economy and a population that is still, like its 19th-Century forebears, predominately patriotic, Constitutionalist, Christian, liberty-loving, and traditional.

The photographs in this book, however, will continue to serve as a reminder of what can happen when progressives, particularly left-wing Yankees, gain political control; mute but powerful imagery that will forever stand as the primary legacy of *The Unholy Crusade* waged by the Liberal North against a peaceful agrarian people: the Conservative South.

Lochlainn Seabrook
Nashville, Tennessee, USA
December 2016

ALABAMA

Ruins of Fort Morgan at the mouth of Mobile Bay, AL, looking southeast. Circa 1861-1869.

Ruins of Fort Morgan at the mouth of Mobile Bay, AL, looking southwest. Circa 1861-1869.

Ruins of a railroad bridge across the Tennessee River, Bridgeport, AL. A temporary pontoon bridge is under construction. Circa 1863.

GEORGIA

A group of Union soldiers (Michigan Regiment) in the act of tearing up railroad track, Atlanta, GA. The remains of the destroyed Atlanta Depot can be seen rear right. Circa 1863-1864.

Another view of the ruins of the railroad depot, Atlanta, GA. Circa 1864.

Ruins of Fort McAllister with a trench filled with chevaux-de-frise, near Savannah, GA. December 1864.

Ruins of private homes, Savannah, GA. 1865.

Ruins of private homes, Savannah, GA. 1865.

More house ruins, Savannah, GA. 1865.

Ruins of private homes, Savannah, GA. 1865.

Ruins of a private home, Savannah, GA. 1865.

Ruins of private homes, Savannah, GA. 1865.

Ruins of the train depot, Atlanta, GA. November 1864.

Ruins of Rolling Mill and a Confederate ordnance train on the Georgia Central Railroad, Atlanta, GA. 1864.

Ruins of buildings and "Sherman's Sentinels," Atlanta, GA. 1864.

Damage to a wall at Fort Pulaski, Savannah, GA. Circa 1934.

The Ponder House, damaged by Union shelling, Atlanta, GA. 1864.

Damaged home of John Ross and family, near Rossville Gap, GA. Circa 1861-1865.

Union General William T. Sherman's men destroying the city railroad before the evacuation of Atlanta, GA. 1864.

Another view of the destruction of the rails by Sherman's men, Atlanta, GA. 1864.

Southern refugees at the train depot preparing to flee the city just prior to Sherman's "March to the Sea," Atlanta, GA. 1864.

"Sherman's Neckties": Southern railroad pried up, twisted, piled, and burned by Sherman and his men on their way through Georgia. November to December 1864.

LOUISIANA

View of the damaged interior of Port Hudson, LA, after siege in July 1863.

Private homes purposefully burned to the ground in 1862 by Union troops, Baton Rouge, LA.

Ruins of private homes, New Orleans, LA.

SOUTH CAROLINA

Looking south down Meeting St., Charleston, SC. In the foreground are the ruins of St. Michael's Church, the Mills House, Central Church, and the Theater. Circa 1865.

Another view on Meeting Street, Charleston, SC. Here we see the ruins of Circular Church, as well as St. Philips Church (behind it). On the right are the ruins of Secession Hall. Circa 1865.

Another view looking south down Meeting St., Charleston, SC. Toward the back are the ruins of St. Michael's Church and the Mills House. In the foreground are the ruins of the Circular Church and the Theater. 1865.

Ruins of the Roman Catholic Church, Charleston, SC. Circa 1865.

The interior of Fort Moultrie, near Charleston, SC, showing the ruins of the sally port and supporting walls. 1865.

Ruined Blakely gun carriage in the street and damaged private homes, South Battery, Charleston, SC. Circa 1865.

Rear view of the ruins of the Cathedral of St. John and St. Finbar, Charleston, SC. Circa 1865.

Front view of the ruins of the Cathedral of St. John and St. Finbar, Charleston, SC. Circa 1865.

A view of the ruins of the Circular Church (left), St. Philip's Church (center), and Secession Hall (right), Charleston, SC. Circa 1865.

The 19th-Century title of this photo is "The Ruins of the Sister Churches, Charleston, SC." Circa 1865.

Photograph of the interior of Fort Sumter, Charleston, SC. Visible is a fortified enclosure on the parapet, gabions (used for reinforcements), and the remains of a casemate. April 1865.

Ruins of Fort Sumter, Charleston Harbor, SC. Visible is a damaged wall of casemates, a shattered flag staff, and rubble. April 1861.

View from the Circular Church at 150 Meeting St., Charleston, SC, showing bombed out buildings, stores, homes, and debris. Circa 1861-1865.

View from the Mills House up Meeting Street, with the ruins of the Circular Church on the right in the midst of repair, Charleston, SC. April 1865.

The Mills House and surrounding ruins, Charleston, SC. April 1865.

A view of the ruins of the North Eastern Railroad Depot, Charleston, SC. April 1865.

Ruins of the interior of Fort Sumter, Charleston Harbor, SC. 1861.

Ruins of the interior of Fort Sumter, Charleston Harbor, SC, with one of the garrison's four Columbiads under debris on the left. 1861.

Interior view of the ruins of the Cathedral of St. John and St. Finbar at Broad and Legare Streets, Charleston, SC. Circa 1865.

Another front view of the ruins of the Cathedral of St. John and St. Finbar, Charleston, SC. Circa 1865.

View looking east on Broad St., Charleston, SC, with the ruins of the Cathedral of St. John and St. Finbar on the left. St. Michael's Church can be seen on the right (center). Circa 1865.

Ruins of the Circular Church and Secession Hall on Meeting St., Charleston, SC. Circa 1865.

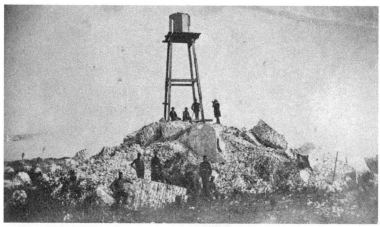

View of the observation tower sitting on top of the ruins of the lighthouse at Morris Island, SC. Circa 1861-1865.

Another view of the ruins of the North Eastern Railway Depot, Charleston, SC. Circa April 1865.

Ruins of Circular Church and Secession Hall, Charleston, SC. April 1865.

Closeup view of the ruins of Circular Church, Charleston, SC. 1865.

Bombed out interior of the Roman Catholic Church, Charleston, SC. April 1865.

Another interior view of the ruins of the Roman Catholic Church, Charleston, SC. April 1865.

Doorway blown apart, Roman Catholic Church, Charleston, SC. April 1865.

Yet another view of the ruins of the Northeastern Railroad Depot, Charleston, SC. 1865.

Ruins of Circular Church, Charleston, SC. December 1861.

Interior view of the ruins of Circular Church, Charleston, SC. Circa 1861-1865.

Another view of the ruins of the Catholic Church, Charleston, SC. April 1865.

Interior ruins of Circular Church, Charleston, SC. Circa 1861-1865.

Ruins of the Old Spanish Fort, Smith's Plantation, Port Royal Island, SC. Circa 1863-1865.

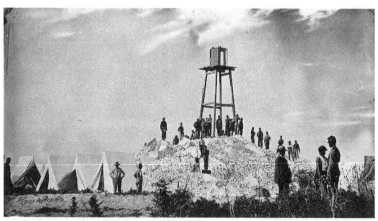

Another view of the ruins of the Charleston Lighthouse, Morris Island, SC. July or August 1863.

City ruins, Charleston, SC. 1865.

City ruins, Meeting St., looking south, Charleston, SC. 1865.

Bombed Southern cemetery, Charleston, SC. 1865.

Ruins of private homes, Charleston, SC. Circa 1863-1865.

Ruins, probably of Fort Sumter, Charleston, SC.
Circa 1863-1865.

Another view of the ruins of Circular Church, Charleston, SC.
Circa 1861-1865.

Exterior of Fort Sumter showing ruins of artillery along the shoreline, Charleston, SC. March 1865.

Ruins of the graveyard of Circular Church, with Secession Hall in the background, Charleston, SC. April 1865.

Damaged sally port, Fort Moultrie, Sullivan's Island, Charleston, SC. 1865.

Interior ruins of Fort Sumter, showing damaged sally port, Charleston Harbor, SC. 1865.

Shoreline view of some of the rubble and ruins at Fort Sumter, Charleston, SC. 1865.

Drawing of the interior ruins of Fort Sumter, with the Confederate Second National Flag flying, Charleston Harbor, SC, by John Ross Key. January 7, 1864.

Interior ruins, Fort Sumter, Charleston, SC. September 8, 1863.

Interior ruins, Fort Sumter, Charleston, SC. September 8, 1863.

Interior ruins, Fort Sumter, Charleston, SC. September 8, 1863.

Interior ruins, Fort Sumter, Charleston, SC. September 8, 1863.

Another view down Meeting St., Charleston, SC. 1865.

Ruins of another Blakely rifled cannon, this one in an open pit on the Battery, Charleston, SC. March 1865.

City ruins near the Mills House, Charleston, SC. 1865.

Ruins of Fort Sumter from sandbar, Charleston Harbor, SC. April 1865.

Remnants of a Blakely gun showing its demolished carriage, Charleston, SC. 1865.

Ruins of Circular Church, Charleston, SC. Circa 1861-1865.

Interior view of the ruins of Fort Sumter, Charleston, SC. Circa 1863.

Another view of the ruins of Fort Sumter from nearby sandbar, Charleston Harbor, SC. Circa 1865.

View of the remnants of an exterior wall after bombardment, Fort Sumter, Charleston Harbor, SC. Circa 1865.

Damaged north face, Fort Sumter, Charleston Harbor, SC. 1865.

Destruction in downtown Charleston, SC. 1865.

Damaged graveyard and monuments of Circular Church, Charleston, SC. Circa 1865.

Damaged palmetto fortifications on the channel side of
Fort Sumter, Charleston Harbor, SC. Circa March 1865.

Damaged buildings looking east from the corner of East Bay St.,
Charleston, SC. Circa 1865.

City damage showing the Old Post Office and the last standing palmetto tree in town, Charleston, SC. Circa 1865.

Remains of a Confederate battery, Charleston, SC. 1865.

City damage, Charleston, SC. Circa 1865.

The damaged Mills House, with Hibernian Hall on the left, Charleston, SC. Circa 1865.

Ruins of private homes, Charleston, SC. April 1865.

Shell damage on Meeting St., Charleston, SC. Circa 1861-1865.

Results of city bombardment showing damage to Dr. Gadsden's house, Charleston, SC. Note remains of homes and churches on left. April 1865.

Ruined interior of Fort Wagner, Morris Island, Charleston Harbor, SC. Circa 1863-1865.

Photograph of the ruins of the Confederate Beacon House, Morris Island, Charleston, SC. Circa 1863-1865.

Interior view of Fort Sumter showing debris and bursted gun, Charleston Harbor, SC. 1865.

A drawing by William Waud of the burning of Columbia, SC, by Union General William T. Sherman on February 17, 1865. Terrorized women and children can be seen fleeing the flames as Yankee soldiers look on. April 8, 1865.

City ruins, Charleston, SC. Circa 1861-1865.

TENNESSEE

Rock Creek Falls on Lookout Mountain, TN, an area severely damaged by the War. Circa 1863 or 1864.

U.S. engineers on a bombed out salient at Fort Sanders, Knoxville, TN. Circa 1863 or 1864.

Ruins of a private home, Knoxville, TN.

VIRGINIA

Ruins of the Arsenal Grounds, Richmond, VA, with remnants of Confederate shot and shell. Circa 1865.

A view of the Lynchburg Canal and Haxall Flour Mills, Richmond, VA. Behind them can be seen the ruins of the Gallego Mills. April 1865.

Ruins of the Richmond and Petersburg Railroad Depot, Richmond, VA. The debris of a demolished locomotive can be seen scattered about. April 1865.

Looking east from the Canal Basin, Richmond, VA, we see the burnt district, with the ruins of the Gallego Flour Mills in the back. 1865.

View across the James River from Richmond, VA, of the Petersburg and Richmond Railroad Bridge, bombed by Union forces. Circa 1864-1866.

View of the ruins of the State Arsenal, Richmond, VA., with the canal in the foreground. Circa 1861-1865.

The Victorian title for this photograph is "Richmond in Ruins." A more appropriate title would be: "The Liberals' Idea of 'Preserving the Union.'" It shows Richmond's burnt district with the James River in the background. Circa 1865.

The Lynchburg Canal with the ruins of the Danville Railroad Depot, Richmond, VA. April 1865.

Another view of the canal and the ruins of the State Arsenal, Richmond, VA. April 1865.

Looking southwest across ruins in the burnt district, Richmond, VA. Gamble Hill is on the horizon. Circa 1865.

Ruins of Richmond, VA. Circa 1861-1865.

Ruins on Carey St., Richmond, VA. April 1865.

Businesses and homes in ruins, Richmond, VA. May 1865.

Ruins of Mayo's Bridge with the city in the background, Richmond, VA. April 1865.

Brick ruins of St. John's Episcopal Church, "the oldest church in America," built in 1728, Hampton, VA. Circa 1862.

Ruins of the Norfolk Navy Yard, Norfolk, VA. Circa 1864-1865.

Ruins of a stone bridge at Bull Run, just north of Manassas, VA. Circa 1862-1865.

View of the James River and the ruins of the Petersburg Railroad Bridge (center), Richmond, VA. Circa 1861-1865.

Photograph of city ruins with stacks of cannonballs near the center, Richmond, VA. April 1865.

Ruins of Gallego Flour Mills on the James River, Richmond, VA. Circa 1861-1865.

Ruins of the railroad yard, Richmond, VA. Circa 1865.

Another view of the ruins of America's oldest church, St. John's Episcopal Church, as seen from the west end, Hampton, VA. Circa 1862.

A distant view of the demolished St. John's Episcopal Church amidst street after street of surrounding city ruins, Hampton, VA. July 2, 1862.

Ruins of Gaines' Mill, Hanover County, VA. April 1865.

Mass destruction at Manassas Junction, VA, showing a rail turntable on the Orange and Alexandria Railroad. Circa 1862-1865.

Ruins at the corner of Carey and Governor Streets, Richmond, VA. May 1865.

Ruins of a paper mill, and also a railroad bridge (left), Richmond, VA. Circa 1865.

Another view of the ruins of the Richmond and Petersburg Railroad Bridge over the James River, Richmond, VA. April 1865.

Ruins at Chancellorsville, VA. Date unknown.

Another view of the ruins of the State Arsenal, Richmond, VA. Circa April 1863.

A recent photograph of the ruins of Spring Hill, destroyed during the Battle of Petersburg, VA, June 15-18, 1864. Circa 1980-2006.

Soldiers bathing in the North Anna River, VA, with the ruins of a railroad bridge in the background. May 1864.

Another view of the ruins of the State Arsenal on the James River, Richmond, VA. April 1865.

Ruins of Gallego Flour Mills on the Kanawha Canal, Richmond, VA. 1865.

A wide shot of the ruins of the State Arsenal and the Richmond and Petersburg Railroad Bridge, Richmond, VA. 1865.

View of the waterwheel amidst the ruins of Gallego Mills, Richmond, VA. April 1865.

Ruins of the Richmond and Danville Railroad Bridge, with the destroyed city in the background, Richmond, VA. April 1865.

Another view of the ruins of the Richmond and Petersburg Railroad Bridge, Richmond, VA. April 1865.

A later view of the ruins of the State Arsenal, Richmond, VA. April 1865.

View of bombed buildings and the ruins of the Richmond and Petersburg Railroad Bridge, Richmond, VA. April 1865.

Ruins of the State Arsenal with Pratt's Castle in the distant background, Richmond, VA. April 1865.

Ruins of the White Sulphur Springs Hotel, Warrenton, VA. September 1863.

African-Americans on an island in the James River, with the ruins of the Richmond and Petersburg Railroad Bridge behind them. April 1865.

The original caption of this Victorian photo reads: "Ruins of Hotel at Fauquier Springs [Warrenton], VA. Circa 1862-1869.

Another view of the ruins of the Gallego Flour Mills, Richmond, VA.
April 1865.

Ruins of Mayo's Bridge, Richmond, VA. 1865.

Another view of the ruins of the Richmond and Danville Railroad Bridge with damaged covered bridge on left, Richmond, VA. April 1865.

City ruins, Richmond, VA. April 1865.

Ruins of the State Arsenal, Richmond, VA. April 1865.

The Battlefield of Manassas, VA (July 1861), with demolished stone bridge. March 1862.

Ruins of Mrs. Judith Henry's home, near Manassas, VA. March 1862.

Ruins of the White House at White House Landing, VA. 1862.

Ruins of a railroad bridge at Blackburn's Ford, near Manassas, VA. 1862.

Ruins of the railroad bridge, Harpers Ferry, VA. Circa 1860-1865.

Ruins of private homes, Charles City, VA. June 1864.

View from Gambles Hill, showing general citywide ruination, Richmond, VA. April 1865.

Ruins of Mayo's Bridge and the city, Richmond, VA. April 1865.

Another view of the ruins of the Richmond and Petersburg Railroad Bridge, Richmond, VA. April 1865.

View from the south bank of the James River of the ruins of the Richmond and Petersburg Railroad Bridge, as well as general city destruction, Richmond, VA. April 1865.

Ruins of the Gallego Flour Mills, Richmond, VA. April 1865.

Ruins of the city paper mill, with demolished paper-making equipment in the foreground, Richmond, VA. April 1865.

Another view of the destroyed paper mill and its waterwheel, Richmond, VA. 1865.

Ruins of the Southern Express Office, Carey St., Richmond, VA. 1865.

Ruins of the Exchange Bank, Main St., Richmond, VA. April 1865.

Though surrounded by ruins, the city's Custom House survived largely intact, Richmond VA. Bricks from the demolished structures are being gathered for use in reconstruction. April 1865.

Drawing of the ruins of a bridge over the Shenandoah River, Loudon Heights, VA, by Alfred R. Waud. 1864.

Ruins of private homes, as well as a demolished locomotive and railroad bridge across the Appomattox River, in the vicinity of Petersburg, VA. April 1865.

Another view of the ruins of the Richmond and Petersburg Railroad Bridge, Richmond, VA. April 1865.

Ruins of private homes, Petersburg, VA. April 1865.

Ruins of private homes, Petersburg, VA. April 3, 1865.

Ruins of a stone bridge near Manassas, VA. March 1862.

Ruins along the canal, Richmond, VA. April 1865.

More ruins along the city canal, Richmond, VA. April 1865.

Ruins of a tobacco warehouse, Richmond, VA. April 1865.

Destroyed train amidst the ruins of the Richmond and Petersburg Railroad Depot, Richmond, VA. April 1865.

Another view of the ruins of the Richmond and Petersburg Railroad Depot, Richmond, VA. April 1865.

City ruins, Richmond, VA. April 1865.

Ruins of the Richmond and Danville Railroad Bridge, Richmond, VA. April 1865.

Ruins of the bridge on the Richmond and York River Railroad, destroyed by Union soldiers May 17, 1862, VA. May 1862.

Ruins of the bridge at Germanna Ford, Rapidan River, VA. May 4, 1864.

Another view of the city ruins, this one looking down the James River, Richmond, VA. April 1865.

City ruins, Richmond, VA. April 1865.

Another view of the ruins of the Richmond and Petersburg Railroad Bridge, Richmond, VA. April 1865.

Drawing of the ruins of the Acquia Creek and Fredericksburg Railroad Bridge over Potomac Creek, by Edwin Forbes. May 10, 1862.

Another view of the ruins of the State Arsenal, Richmond, VA. 1865.

Ruins of the woolen mill, Petersburg, VA. May 1865.

Another one of the South's thousands of streets filled with the ruins of private homes, probably Fredericksburg, VA. Circa 1862-1869.

Interior view of the demolished Gallego Mills, Richmond, VA. April 1865.

Drawing entitled "The Ruins of Hampton, Virginia," by William McIlvaine. 1862.

City ruins with wrecked cannon in foreground, Richmond, VA. 1865.

Ruins of another Southern railway bridge, Richmond, VA. April 1865.

City ruins as far as the eye can see, Richmond, VA. April 1865.

Ruins of the Phillips House, near Falmouth, VA. Circa 1861-1865.

Part of the burnt district, Richmond, VA. 1865.

Ruins of a railroad bridge, Richmond, VA. April 1865.

Widespread city ruins, Richmond, VA. April 1865.

Ruins of the Richmond and Petersburg Railroad Bridge, Richmond, VA. April 1865.

Ruins of the Lacy House, Battle of the Wilderness, VA. 1865.

Ruins of private homes, Chancellorsville, VA. 1865.

Ruins of the Henry House, Battle of Manassas, VA. Circa 1861-1865.

Another view of the ruins of the railroad bridge at Blackburn's Ford, VA. Circa 1861-1865.

Another view of the ruins of the stone bridge at the site of the Battle of Manassas, VA. Circa 1861-1865.

Another view of the ruins of the Richmond and Petersburg Railroad Bridge, Richmond, VA. April 1865.

City ruins on Carey St., Richmond, VA. Circa 1861-1865.

City ruins on the Canal Basin, Richmond, VA. April 1865.

Ruins of the Gallego Flour Mills, Richmond, VA. April 1865.

Another view of the ruins of the railroad bridge at Blackburn's Ford, VA. Circa 1861-1865.

Ruins of a stone bridge on the Manassas battlefield, VA. Circa 1861-1865.

City ruins on Carey St., Richmond, VA. April 1865.

City ruins on Carey St., Richmond, VA. April 1865.

Canal ruins, Richmond, VA. April 1865.

Another view of the ruins of the Gallego Flour Mills, Richmond, VA. Circa 1861-1865.

City ruins near the Tredegar Iron Works, Richmond, VA. April 1865.

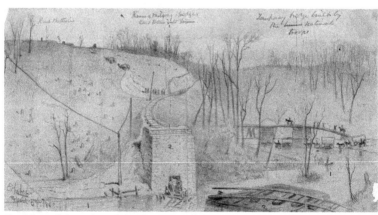

Drawing of the ruins of the Orange and Alexandria Railroad Bridge over Bull Run, located near Union Mills, VA, by Edwin Forbes. April 5, 1862.

Another view of the ruins of the paper mill, Richmond, VA, 1865.

Interior ruins at Fort Rice, near Petersburg, VA. April 2, 1865.

Drawing of the city ruins of Richmond, VA, by A. W. Warren. April 3, 1865.

City view across Canal Basin, showing the Capitol and Custom House and ruins in the background, Richmond, VA. April 1865.

A wide city view from the south side of Canal Basin, Richmond, VA. 1865.

Ruins of fortifications in the midst of the James River, Drewry's Bluff, Richmond, VA. Circa 1861-1865.

Another view of the ruins in the middle of the James River, Drewry's Bluff, Richmond, VA. Circa 1861-1865.

City ruins, Richmond, VA. Circa 1861-1865.

Drawing of female residents on their way to receive government rations amidst the bombed out downtown area, Richmond, VA, by Alfred R. Waud. The proudly Confederate women are turning up their noses at the Yankee officer walking past. 1865.

Drawing of the ruins of the Norfolk Navy Yard, Norfolk, VA, by Alfred R. Waud. Circa May 9, 1862.

Ruins of the Belle Isle covered railroad bridge from the south bank of the James River, Richmond, VA. 1865.

Drawing of Martinsburg, VA (WV), by Alfred R. Waud, showing the ruins of the Depot, as well as the Square, the Barricades, the Court House, Hoge's House, and the Opequan River. Circa December 3, 1864.

City ruins, Richmond, VA. April 1865.

City ruins, Richmond, VA. April 1865.

City ruins, Richmond, VA. April 1865.

Damaged mills in Manchester, Richmond, VA. April 1865.

Ruins of private homes, Fredericksburg, VA. 1862.

Ruins of the Tredegar Iron Works, showing footbridge to Neilson's Island on left, Richmond, VA. Circa 1861-1865.

Ruins on the James River, City Point, VA. Circa 1861-1865.

City ruins showing the burnt district, as seen from Gambles Hill, Richmond, VA. April 1865.

Repair being done to ruined High Bridge, which crosses the Appomattox River near Farmville, VA. 1865.

Damaged private homes, Fredericksburg, VA. May 19, 1864.

Shelled and damaged private home, Petersburg, VA. 1865.

Damaged private home, Petersburg, VA. 1865.

Ruins of private homes, Petersburg, VA. 1865.

The Moore House, damaged by shot and shell, Yorktown, VA. May 1862.

Mathews' House, damaged during the Battle of Manassas, VA. March 1862.

Damaged Dunlop House on Bollingbrook St., Petersburg, VA. Circa 1861-1865.

Damaged private home being used as a Union field hospital on the battlefield of Fair Oaks, VA. June 1862.

Shot and shell damage to a private home in the Marye's Heights section of Fredericksburg, VA. The stone wall in front of the house has been obliterated. May 15, 1864.

The Custom House with destroyed homes in the foreground, Richmond, VA. April 1865.

Drawing of Troops marching past a damaged bridge at Germanna Ford during the Mine Run Campaign, VA, by Alfred R. Waud. Circa December 1863.

Damaged private home on the battlefield of Cedar Mountain, VA, where Confederate General Charles S. Winder perished. 1862.

Bombed private homes along a street in Fredericksburg, VA. 1862.

Bombed railroad bridge on the North Ana River, VA. May 26, 1864.

Drawing of the destruction of a train crossing a bridge over the Chickahominy River, VA, by Alfred R. Waud. June 1862.

Drawing of Yankee troops destroying the communication lines of Confederate General Robert E. Lee, in Virginia, by Alfred R. Waud. June 1864.

Blacks under Union command using levers to tear up Confederate rails in northern Virginia. What did such useless destruction have to do with either "preserving the Union" or "abolishing slavery"? Circa 1862 or 1863.

Black Union workers twisting and destroying Confederate railroad in Northern Virginia. Circa 1862 or 1863.

Bullet-riddled smokestack from the Confederate ram *Virginia*, Richmond, VA. Circa 1861-1865.

More city ruins, Richmond, VA. 1865.

Arlington House, the home of Confederate General Robert E. Lee, Arlington, VA. After forcing Lee's wife and children into the street, Union soldiers ransacked and pillaged the beautiful home of its valuables, then posed arrogantly for this photo in the front yard. June 29, 1864.

Confederate caisson destroyed by Yankee shells, Fredericksburg, VA. Dead horses lie among the carnage. May 3, 1863.

Interior of the Dunlop House showing damage made by Union shelling, Petersburg, VA. 1865.

Photo of the city gas works damaged by Yankee artillery, Petersburg, VA. May 1865.

City ruins, burnt district, Richmond, VA. 1865.

City ruins, Richmond, VA. April 1865.

View of the remnants of the railroad station at Manassas Junction, VA. March 1862.

The damaged Confederate gunboat *Teaser*, captured by Yanks on July 4, 1862, James River, VA. July 1862.

The Paymaster's Quarters, Harpers Ferry, VA, extensively damaged during Lincoln's War (and later repaired). Erected in 1847, it was part of the Harpers Ferry Armory. 1958.

Damaged Lutheran Church, Sharpsburg, VA. 1911.

Demolished private home, Fredericksburg, VA, where it is said that "every house became a target" of Union troops. 1911.

Wilderness Church, whose roof was riddled with bullets during the Battle of Chancellorsville, VA. 1911.

Homes destroyed during the Chancellorsville campaign. 1911.

City, rail, and train ruins, Richmond, VA. 1865.

Stored shot and canister amid the ruins of the Arsenal grounds, Richmond, VA. 1865.

Stolen Confederate artillery on the docks at Rocketts Landing, Richmond, VA. 1865.

A distant view of the ruins around Canal Basin, Richmond, VA. Circa 1861-1865.

Demolished Southern locomotive, Richmond, VA. 1865.

Ruins, Tredegar Iron Works, Richmond, VA. April 1865.

MISCELLANEOUS

Ruins of a private home, location unknown. Circa 1861-1865.

A Union battery near Vicksburg, VA. Federal besiegers such as these were
the cause of much of the damage in the South.

Confederate guns captured by the Union in Georgia.

Union guns, like these powerful 13 inch siege mortars, destroyed both countless structures and human lives across the South. For what?

Southern garrisons, like Fort Pulaski (pictured here), took the brunt of the Liberals' savagery, but untold numbers of homes, businesses, schools, courthouses, hospitals, and even libraries were also destroyed. Why?

Two of the South's greatest generals: Joseph E. Johnston (left), Robert E. Lee (right). 1869.

Dock view from the south side of the James River, across from Rocketts Landing, Richmond, VA. 1865.

Confederate guns, like this 10-inch Columbiad at Fort Walker, Hilton Head, SC, were also partly responsible for some of the damage in the South. However, this purposeful demolition was only necessary to prevent supplies and structures from being captured by the enemy. Thus none of this would have occurred had not Lincoln called for the invasion of the Confederacy in April 1861. The responsibility for all of the death and destruction of the War ultimately lies with America's sixteenth president.

Confederate dead gathered for burial July 5, 1863, Gettysburg, PA. The most unpardonable destruction of Lincoln's unholy crusade was not homes, barns, stores, and churches. These can all be rebuilt. It was the toll on human life, which meddling, heartless, Liberal Yankee troops swept away like dry leaves before a firestorm.

Confederate dead on the Hagerstown Rd., Antietam, MD, September 1862. Southern historians estimate that some 2 million Southerners died as a result of Lincoln's War: 1 million European-Americans and 1 million African-Americans.

Big government Liberal Abraham Lincoln, who tried to destroy the government and Constitution created by the Founding Generation.

Small government Conservative Jefferson Davis, who tried to preserve the government and Constitution created by the Founding Generation.

NOTES

1. Woods, p. 47.
2. Burns, pp. 549, 553. As their name indicates, though mainly progressive, fusionists embraced bits and pieces from various other political parties.
3. Seabrook, LW, pp. 73-83, passim.
4. Benson and Kennedy, pp. 145-146.
5. See Jones, TDMV, pp. 144, 200-201, 273.
6. J. M. McPherson, ALATSAR, pp. 23-24.
7. J. M. McPherson, ALATSAR, pp. 5-6.
8. See Seabrook, TAHSR, passim. See also Stephens, ACVOTLW, Vol. 1, pp. 10, 12, 148, 150-151, 157-158, 161, 170, 192, 206, 210, 215, 219, 221-222, 238-240, 258-260, 288, 355, 360, 370, 382-384, 516, 575-576, 583, 587; Vol. 2, pp. 28-30, 32-33, 88, 206, 258, 631, 648; Pollard, LC, p. 178; J. H. Franklin, pp. 101, 111, 130, 149; Nicolay and Hay, ALCW, Vol. 1, p. 627.
9. Rutherford, TOH, p. ix.
10. Muzzey, Vol. 2, p. 140.
11. Stephens, ACVOTLW, Vol. 2, p. 33.
12. "Post-truth politics" is a political environment in which public opinion is shaped by emotion and personal belief rather than objective facts. We can thank the Liberal-controlled media, with its aggressive and largely uneducated bastion of intolerant socialists, communists, and anarchists, for this form of intellectual dishonesty.
13. See e.g., Seabrook, TQJD, pp. 30, 38, 76.
14. See e.g., J. Davis, RFCG, Vol. 1, pp. 55, 422; Vol. 2, pp. 4, 161, 454, 610. Besides using the term "Civil War" himself, President Davis cites numerous other individuals who use it as well.
15. See e.g., Confederate Veteran, March 1912, Vol. 20, No. 3, p. 122.
16. Minutes of the Eighth Annual Meeting, July 1898, p. 87.
17. Selcer, p. 247.
18. Seabrook, AL, p. 434.
19. Seabrook, AL, p. 435.
20. Hall, Smither, and Ousley, pp. 378-379.
21. Stonebraker, pp. 170-171.
22. Gragg, pp. 169-175, 189, 239.
23. Wiley, LBY, p. 203.
24. Fry, p. 99.
25. M. Perry, p. 223.
26. DiLorenzo, RL, pp. 173-174, 178-199.
27. Sherman, Vol. 1, pp. 339-340.
28. Sherman, Vol. 2, p. 119.
29. See Sherman, Vol. 2, pp. 96-136.
30. Gragg, p. 173.
31. As mentioned elsewhere, in all fairness to the Yanks some of this devastation was caused by retreating Confederate forces. But this was done only to prevent supplies from being captured by Union soldiers, an illegal military force that should not have been in the South in the first

place. Civil War Society, p. 16.
32. E. M. Thomas, p. 276.
33. Warner, GB, s.v. "William Tecumseh 'Cump' Sherman."
34. D. Evans, pp. 13, 19-20, 51, 487.
35. ORA, Ser. 1, Vol. 38, Pt. 5, p. 688.
36. Seabrook, AL, p. 432.
37. ORA, Ser. 1, Vol. 32, Pt. 1, p. 176.
38. Seabrook, AL, p. 432.
39. DiLorenzo, RL, p. 185.
40. Wyeth, LGNBF, p. 634; Lytle, p. 271.
41. ORA, Ser. 1, Vol. 32, Pt. 2, p. 498.
42. ORA, Ser. 1, Vol. 44, p. 13.
43. See Sherman, Vol. 2, p. 231.
44. Nicolay and Hay, ALCW, Vol. 2, p. 622.
45. Seabrook, AL, p. 445.
46. Seabrook, AL, p. 445.
47. Nicolay and Hay, ALCW, Vol. 2, p. 563.
48. Sherman, Vol. 2, pp. 227-228.
49. Letter dated September 14, 1865. J. Davis, RFCG, Vol. 2, pp. 710-711.
50. Chesnut, DD, p. 358.
51. Grimsley, p. 182.
52. Bancroft and Dunning, Vol. 3, p. 167.
53. Seabrook, AL, p. 442.
54. My paraphrasal.
55. Daugherty, p. 208.
56. Civil War Society, pp. 80-81; Wyeth, LGNBF, pp. 430-431.
57. Seabrook, ARB, p. 46.
58. ORA, Ser. 1, Vol. 39, Pt. 3, p. 494.
59. ORA, Ser. 1, Vol. 39, Pt. 3, p. 656.
60. Seabrook, ARB, pp. 42-47.
61. McIlwain, pp. 254-255.
62. Seabrook, ARB, pp. 342-347.
63. See Seabrook, NBFATKKK, pp. 52-53.
64. Early, p. 48.
65. ORA, Ser. 1, Vol. 43, Pt. 2, p. 308.
66. Seabrook, AL, p. 443.
67. Douglas, p. 315.
68. ORA, Ser. 1, Vol. 18, Pt. 1, p. 811.
69. ORA, Ser. 1, Vol. 34, Pt. 1, p. 26.
70. ORA, Ser. 1, Vol. 44, p. 741.
71. ORA, Ser. 1, Vol. 8, p. 642.
72. ORA, Ser. 3, Vol. 4, p. 1029.
73. Seabrook, AL, p. 434.
74. Jordan and Pryor, pp. 549-552.
75. See Seabrook, ARB, pp. 345-347.
76. See e.g., J. Davis, RFCG, Vol. 2, pp. 632-633; C. Johnson, p. 157; Lott, pp. 158-159; L. Johnson, p. 188; Grissom, pp. 115-116; Christian, p. 15.
77. Seabrook, AL, p. 349.

204 ↔THE UNHOLY CRUSADE

78. Pollard, SHW, Vol. 2, p. 198; L. Johnson, p. 135. For official reference to Lincoln's "government plantations," see, for example, ORA, Ser. 1, Vol. 26, Pt. 1, p. 764. See also Nicolay and Hay, ALCW, Vol. 2, pp. 471-472.

79. Seabrook, AL, p. 353.

80. Seabrook, AL, pp. 527-543.

81. Seabrook, AL, pp. 536-537.

82. Seabrook, AL, p. 535.

83. Seabrook, AL, pp. 275-308.

84. Seabrook, AL, p. 553.

85. Seabrook, LW, pp. 9-12, 75, 77-99.

86. See Seabrook, ALWAL, passim. Also see supra, 9-13.

87. For a detailed discussion on this topic, see Seabrook, LW, passim.

88. Liberals and other South-haters please note that the Constitution contains no prohibition of secession.

89. Seabrook, AL, p. 75.

90. Seabrook, LW, p. 20.

91. For more on this topic, see Seabrook, C101, passim.

92. Steel, p. 3.

93. J. S. Bowman, ECW, s.v. "Thanks of Congress."

94. Seabrook, AL, p. 446.

95. Christian, pp. 15, 17, 20.

96. Christian, pp. 15-20.

97. Grissom, pp. 117-118.

98. Grissom, p. 117.

99. Seabrook, C101, pp. 79-84.

100. Seabrook, LW, p. 308.

101. Seabrook, EYWTAAAIW, p. 317.

102. Seabrook, LW, p. 33.

103. Seabrook, C101, p. 59; Seabrook, LW, pp. 19-20, 91, 101.

104. Seabrook, EYWTAAAIW, p. 281.

105. See Seabrook, LW, passim.

106. Current, TC, s.v. "Lincoln, Abraham."

107. Stephens, CV, Vol. 2, p. 466; McElroy, p. 319.

BIBLIOGRAPHY

Note: My pro-South readers are to be advised that the majority of the books listed here are anti-South in nature (some extremely so), and were written primarily by liberal elitist, socialist, communist, and Marxist authors who loath the South, and typically the United States and the U.S. Constitution as well. Despite this, as a scholar I find these titles indispensable, for *an honest evaluation of Lincoln's War is not possible without studying both the Southern and the Northern versions*—an attitude, unfortunately, completely lacking among pro-North historians (who read and study only their own version). Still, it must be said that the material contained in these often mean-spirited works is largely the result of a century and a half of Yankee myth, falsehoods, cherry-picking, slander, anti-South propaganda, outright lies, and junk research, as modern pro-North writers merely copy one another's errors without ever looking at the original 19th-Century sources. This type of literature, filled as it is with both misinformation and disinformation, is called "scholarly" and "objective" by pro-North advocates. In the process, the mistakes and lies in these fact-free, fault-ridden, South-shaming, historically inaccurate works have been magnified over the years, and the North's version of the "Civil War" has come to be accepted as the only legitimate one. Indeed, it is now the only one known by most people. That over 95 percent of the titles in my bibliography fall into the anti-South category is simply a reflection of the enormous power and influence that the pro-North movement—our nation's cultural ruling class—has long held over America's educational system, libraries, publishing houses, and media (paper and electronic). My books serve as a small rampart against the overwhelming tide of anti-South Fascists, Liberals, and political elites, all who are working hard to obliterate Southern culture and guarantee that you will never learn the Truth about Lincoln and his War on the Constitution and the American people.

Bancroft, Frederic, and William A. Dunning (eds.). *The Reminiscences of Carl Schurz.* 3 vols. New York, NY: McClure Co., 1909.

Benson, Al, Jr., and Walter Donald Kennedy. *Lincoln's Marxists.* Gretna, LA: Pelican, 2011.

Boyd, James P. *Parties, Problems, and Leaders of 1896: An Impartial Presentation of Living National Questions.* Chicago, IL: Publishers' Union, 1896.

Bowman, John S. (ed.). *The Civil War Day by Day: An Illustrated Almanac of America's Bloodiest War.* 1989. New York, NY: Dorset Press, 1990 ed.

——. *Encyclopedia of the Civil War* (ed.). 1992. North Dighton, MA: JG Press, 2001 ed.

Browder, Earl. *Lincoln and the Communists.* New York, NY: Workers Library Publishers, Inc., 1936.

Bryan, William Jennings. *The First Battle: A Story of the Campaign of 1896.* Chicago, IL: W. B. Conkey Co., 1896.

Burns, James MacGregor. *The Vineyard of Liberty.* New York, NY: Alfred A. Knopf, 1982.

Chesnut, Mary. *A Diary From Dixie: As Written by Mary Boykin Chesnut, Wife of James Chesnut, Jr., United States Senator from South Carolina, 1859-1861, and Afterward an Aide to Jefferson Davis and a Brigadier-General in the Confederate Army.* (Isabella D. Martin and Myrta Lockett Avary, eds.). New York, NY: D. Appleton and Co.,

1905 ed.

Christian, George L. *Abraham Lincoln: An Address Delivered Before R. E. Lee Camp, No. 1 Confederate Veterans at Richmond, VA, October 29, 1909.* Richmond, VA: L. H. Jenkins, 1909.

Civil War Society, The. *Civil War Battles: An Illustrated Encyclopedia.* 1997. New York, NY: Gramercy, 1999 ed.

———. *The Civil War Society's Encyclopedia of the Civil War.* New York, NY: Wings Books, 1997.

Current, Richard N. *The Lincoln Nobody Knows.* 1958. New York, NY: Hill and Wang, 1963 ed.

———. (ed.) *The Confederacy* (Information Now Encyclopedia). 1993. New York, NY: Macmillan, 1998 ed.

Daugherty, James. *Abraham Lincoln.* 1943. New York, NY: Scholastic Book Services, 1966 ed.

Davis, Jefferson. *The Rise and Fall of the Confederate Government.* 2 vols. New York, NY: D. Appleton and Co., 1881.

DiLorenzo, Thomas J. *The Real Lincoln: A New Look at Abraham Lincoln, His Agenda, and an Unnecessary War.* Three Rivers, MI: Three Rivers Press, 2003.

Douglas, Henry Kyd. *I Rode With Stonewall: The War Experiences of the Youngest Member of Jackson's Staff.* 1940. Chapel Hill, NC: University of North Carolina Press, 1968 ed.

Durden, Robert F. *The Gray and the Black: The Confederate Debate on Emancipation.* Baton Rouge, LA: Louisiana State University Press, 1972.

Early, Jubal A. *A Memoir of the Last Year of the War for Independence in the Confederate States of America.* Lynchburg, VA: Charles W. Button, 1867.

Evans, David. *Sherman's Horsemen: Union Cavalry Operations in the Atlanta Campaign.* Bloomington, IN: Indiana University Press, 1996.

Franklin, John Hope. *Reconstruction After the Civil War.* Chicago, IL: University of Chicago Press, 1961.

Fry, Henry Peck. *The Modern Ku Klux Klan.* Boston, MA: Small, Maynard, and Co., 1922.

Gragg, Rod. *The Illustrated Confederate Reader: Extraordinary Eyewitness Accounts by the Civil War's Southern Soldiers and Civilians.* New York, NY: Gramercy Books, 1989.

Greene, Lorenzo Johnston. *The Negro in Colonial New England, 1620-1776.* New York, NY: Columbia University Press, 1942.

Greenhow, Rose O'Neal. *My Imprisonment and the First Year of Abolition Rule at Washington.* London, UK: Richard Bentley, 1863.

Grimsley, Mark. *The Hard Hand of War: Union Military Policy Toward Southern Civilians, 1861-1865.* 1995. Cambridge, UK: Cambridge University Press, 1997 ed.

Grissom, Michael Andrew. *Southern By the Grace of God.* 1988. Gretna, LA: Pelican Publishing Co., 1995 ed.

Hall, Robert Green, Harriet Smither, and Clarence Ousley. *A History of the United States for the Grammar Grades.* Dallas, TX: The Southern Publishing Co., 1920.

Johnson, Clint. *The Politically Incorrect Guide to the South (and Why It Will Rise Again).* Washington, D.C.: Regnery, 2006.

Johnson, Ludwell H. *North Against South: The American Iliad, 1848-1877.* 1978. Columbia, SC: Foundation for American Education, 1993 ed.

Johnstone, Huger William. *Truth of War Conspiracy, 1861.* Idylwild, GA: H. W. Johnstone, 1921.

Jones, John William. *The Davis Memorial Volume; Or Our Dead President, Jefferson Davis and the World's Tribute to His Memory.* Richmond, VA: B. F. Johnson, 1889.

Jordan, Thomas, and John P. Pryor. *The Campaigns of General Nathan Bedford Forrest and of Forrest's Cavalry.* New Orleans, LA: Blelock and Co., 1868.

Lott, Stanley K. *The Truth About American Slavery.* 2004. Clearwater, SC: Eastern Digital Resources, 2005 ed.

Lytle, Andrew Nelson. *Bedford Forrest and His Critter Company.* New York, NY: G. P. Putnam's Sons, 1931.

Magliocca, Gerard N. *The Tragedy of William Jennings Bryan: Constitutional Law and the Politics of Backlash.* New Haven, CT: Yale University Press, 2011.

McCarty, Burke (ed.). *Little Sermons in Socialism by Abraham Lincoln.* Chicago, IL: The Chicago Daily Socialist, 1910.

McElroy, Robert. *Jefferson Davis: The Unreal and the Real.* 1937. New York, NY: Smithmark, 1995 ed.

McIlwain, Christopher Lyle. *Civil War Alabama.* Tuscaloosa, AL: University of Alabama Press, 2016.

McPherson, James M. *Abraham Lincoln and the Second American Revolution.* New York, NY: Oxford University Press, 1991.

Meriwether, Elizabeth Avery (pseudonym, "George Edmonds"). *Facts and Falsehoods Concerning the War on the South, 1861-1865.* Memphis, TN: A. R. Taylor and Co., 1904.

Miller, Francis Trevelyan (ed.). *The Photographic History of the War.* 10 vols. New York, NY: The Review of Reviews Co., 1911.

Minutes of the Eighth Annual Meeting and Reunion of the United Confederate Veterans, Atlanta, GA, July 20-23, 1898. New Orleans, LA: United Confederate Veterans, 1907.

Minutes of the Ninth Annual Meeting and Reunion of the United Confederate Veterans, Charleston, SC, May 10-13, 1899. New Orleans, LA: United Confederate Veterans, 1907.

Minutes of the Twelfth Annual Meeting and Reunion of the United Confederate Veterans, Dallas, TX, April 22-25, 1902. New Orleans, LA: United Confederate Veterans, 1907.

Muzzey, David Saville. *The United States of America: Vol. 1, To the Civil War.* Boston, MA: Ginn and Co., 1922.

——. *The American Adventure: Vol. 2, From the Civil War.* 1924. New York, NY: Harper and Brothers, 1927 ed.

Nicolay, John G., and John Hay (eds.). *Abraham Lincoln: A History.* 10 vols. New York, NY: The Century Co., 1890.

——. *Complete Works of Abraham Lincoln.* 12 vols. 1894. New York, NY: Francis D. Tandy Co., 1905 ed.

——. *Abraham Lincoln: Complete Works.* 12 vols. 1894. New York, NY: The Century Co., 1907 ed.

ORA (full title: *The War of the Rebellion: A Compilation of the Official Records of the Union* and Confederate Armies). 70 vols. Washington, DC: Government Printing Office, 1880.

ORN (full title: Official Records of the Union and Confederate Navies in the War of the Rebellion). 30 vols. Washington, DC: Government Printing Office, 1894.

Perry, Mark. Lift Up Thy Voice: The Grimké Family's Journey From Slaveholders to Civil Rights Leaders. New York, NY: Penguin, 2001.

Pollard, Edward A. Southern History of the War. 2 vols. in 1. New York, NY: Charles B. Richardson, 1866.

——. The Lost Cause. 1867. Chicago, IL: E. B. Treat, 1890 ed.

——. The Lost Cause Regained. New York, NY: G. W. Carlton and Co., 1868.

——. Life of Jefferson Davis, With a Secret History of the Southern Confederacy, Gathered "Behind the Scenes in Richmond." Philadelphia, PA: National Publishing Co., 1869.

Rove, Karl. The Triumph of William McKinley: Why the Election of 1896 Still Matters. New York, NY: Simon and Schuster, 2015.

Rutherford, Mildred Lewis. Truths of History: A Fair, Unbiased, Impartial, Unprejudiced and Conscientious Study of History. Athens, GA: n.p., 1920.

Seabrook, Lochlainn. Abraham Lincoln: The Southern View. 2007. Franklin, TN: Sea Raven Press, 2013 ed.

——. A Rebel Born: A Defense of Nathan Bedford Forrest. 2010. Franklin, TN: Sea Raven Press, 2011 ed.

——. Everything You Were Taught About the Civil War is Wrong, Ask a Southerner! 2010. Franklin, TN: Sea Raven Press, revised 2014 ed.

——. The Quotable Jefferson Davis: Selections From the Writings and Speeches of the Confederacy's First President. Franklin, TN: Sea Raven Press, 2011.

——. Lincolnology: The Real Abraham Lincoln Revealed In His Own Words. Franklin, TN: Sea Raven Press, 2011.

——. The Unquotable Abraham Lincoln: The President's Quotes They Don't Want You To Know! Franklin, TN: Sea Raven Press, 2011.

——. The Great Impersonator: 99 Reasons to Dislike Abraham Lincoln. Spring Hill, TN: Sea Raven Press, 2012.

——. The Alexander H. Stephens Reader: Excerpts From the Works of a Confederate Founding Father. Spring Hill, TN: Sea Raven Press, 2013.

——. Everything You Were Taught About American Slavery War is Wrong, Ask a Southerner! Spring Hill, TN: Sea Raven Press, 2015.

——. Confederacy 101: Amazing Facts You Never Knew About America's Oldest Political Tradition. Spring Hill, TN: Sea Raven Press, 2015.

——. The Great Yankee Coverup: What the North Doesn't Want You to Know About Lincoln's War! Spring Hill, TN: Sea Raven Press, 2015.

——. Slavery 101: Amazing Facts You Never Knew About America's "Peculiar Institution." Spring Hill, TN: Sea Raven Press, 2015.

——. Confederacy 101: Amazing Facts You Never Knew About America's Oldest Political Tradition. Spring Hill, TN: Sea Raven Press, 2015.

——. The Great Yankee Coverup: What the North Doesn't Want You to Know About Lincoln's War! Spring Hill, TN: Sea Raven Press, 2015.

——. Confederate Flag Facts: What Every American Should Know About Dixie's Southern Cross.

Spring Hill, TN: Sea Raven Press, 2016.

——. *Everything You Were Taught About African-Americans and the Civil War is Wrong, Ask a Southerner!* Spring Hill, TN: Sea Raven Press, 2016.

——. *Nathan Bedford Forrest and the Ku Klux Klan: Yankee Myth, Confederate Fact.* Spring Hill, TN: Sea Raven Press, 2016.

——. *Lincoln's War: The Real Cause, the Real Winner, the Real Loser.* Spring Hill, TN: Sea Raven Press, 2016.

——. *Abraham Lincoln Was a Liberal, Jefferson Davis Was a Conservative: The Missing Key to Understanding the American Civil War.* Spring Hill, TN: Sea Raven Press, 2017.

Selcer, Richard F. *Civil War America, 1850-1875.* New York, NY: Facts on File, 2006.

Sherman, William Tecumseh. *Memoirs of General William T. Sherman.* 2 vols. 1875. New York, NY: D. Appleton and Co., 1891 ed.

Stephens, Alexander Hamilton. *Speech of Mr. Stephens, of Georgia, on the War and Taxation.* Washington, D.C.: J & G. Gideon, 1848.

——. *A Constitutional View of the Late War Between the States; Its Causes, Character, Conduct and Results.* 2 vols. Philadelphia, PA: National Publishing, Co., 1870.

——. *Recollections of Alexander H. Stephens: His Diary Kept When a Prisoner at Fort Warren, Boston Harbour, 1865.* New York, NY: Doubleday, Page, and Co., 1910.

Steel, Samuel Augustus. *The South Was Right.* Columbia, SC: R. L. Bryan Co., 1914.

Stonebraker, J. Clarence. *The Unwritten South: Cause, Progress and Results of the Civil War - Relics of Hidden Truth After Forty Years.* Seventh ed., n.p., 1908.

Thomas, Emory M. *The Confederate Nation: 1861-1865.* New York, NY: Harper and Row, 1979.

Thompson, Holland. *The New South: A Chronicle of Social and Industrial Evolution.* New Haven, CT: Yale University Press, 1920.

Warner, Ezra J. *Generals in Gray: Lives of the Confederate Commanders. 1959.* Baton Rouge, LA: Louisiana State University Press, 1989 ed.

——. *Generals in Blue: Lives of the Union Commanders.* 1964. Baton Rouge, LA: Louisiana State University Press, 2006 ed.

Watts, Peter. *A Dictionary of the Old West.* 1977. New York, NY: Promontory Press, 1987 ed.

Wiley, Bell Irvin. *Southern Negroes: 1861-1865.* 1938. New Haven, CT: Yale University Press, 1969 ed.

——. *The Life of Johnny Reb: The Common Soldier of the Confederacy.* 1943. Baton Rouge, LA: Louisiana State University Press, 1978 ed.

——. *The Plain People of the Confederacy.* 1943. Columbia, SC: University of South Carolina, 2000 ed.

——. *The Life of Billy Yank: The Common Soldier of the Union.* 1952. Baton Rouge, LA: Louisiana State University Press, 2001 ed.

Woods, Thomas E., Jr. *The Politically Incorrect Guide to American History.* Washington, D.C.: Regnery, 2004.

Wyeth, John Allan. *Life of General Nathan Bedford Forrest.* 1899. New York, NY: Harper and Brothers, 1908 ed.

INDEX

MEET THE AUTHOR

OCHLAINN SEABROOK, a Kentucky Colonel and the winner of the prestigious Jefferson Davis Historical Gold Medal for his "masterpiece," *A Rebel Born: A Defense of Nathan Bedford Forrest*, is an unreconstructed Southern historian, award-winning author, Civil War scholar, Bible authority, and traditional Southern Agrarian of Scottish, English, Irish, Dutch, Welsh, German, and Italian extraction.

A child prodigy, Seabrook is today a true Renaissance Man whose occupational titles also include encyclopedist, lexicographer, musician, artist, graphic designer, genealogist, photographer, and award-winning poet. Also a songwriter and a screenwriter, he has a 40 year background in historical nonfiction writing and is a member of the Sons of Confederate Veterans, the Civil War Trust, and the National Grange.

Due to similarities in their writing styles, ideas, and literary works, Seabrook is often referred to as the "new Shelby Foote," the "Southern Joseph Campbell," and the "American Robert Graves" (his English cousin). Seabrook coined the terms "South-shaming" and "Lincolnian liberalism," and holds the world's record for writing the most books on Nathan Bedford Forrest: nine. In addition, Seabrook is the first Civil War scholar to connect the early American nickname for the U.S., "The Confederate States of America," with the Southern Confederacy that arose eight decades later, and the first to note that in 1860 the party platforms of the two major political parties were the opposite of what they are today (Victorian Democrats were conservatives, Victorian Republicans were liberals).

Above, Colonel Lochlainn Seabrook, award-winning Civil War scholar and unreconstructed Southern historian. America's most popular and prolific pro-South author, his many books have introduced hundreds of thousands to the truth about the War for Southern Independence. He coined the phrase "South-shaming" and holds the world's record for writing the most books on Nathan Bedford Forrest: nine.

The grandson of an Appalachian coal-mining family, Seabrook is a seventh-generation Kentuckian, co-chair of the Jent/Gent Family Committee (Kentucky), founder and director of the Blakeney Family Tree Project, and a board member of the Friends of Colonel Benjamin E. Caudill.

Seabrook's literary works have been endorsed by leading authorities, museum curators, award-winning historians, bestselling authors, celebrities, noted scientists, well respected educators, TV show hosts and producers, renowned military artists, esteemed Southern organizations, and distinguished academicians from around the world.

Seabrook has authored over 50 popular adult books on the American Civil War,

American and international slavery, the U.S. Confederacy (1781), the Southern Confederacy (1861), religion, theology and thealogy, Jesus, the Bible, the Apocrypha, the Law of Attraction, alternative health, spirituality, ghost stories, the paranormal, ufology, social issues, and cross-cultural studies of the family and marriage. His Confederate biographies, pro-South studies, genealogical monographs, family histories, military encyclopedias, self-help guides, and etymological dictionaries have received wide acclaim.

Seabrook's eight children's books include a Southern guide to the Civil War, a biography of Nathan Bedford Forrest, a dictionary of religion and myth, a rewriting of the King Arthur legend (which reinstates the original pre-Christian motifs), two bedtime stories for preschoolers, a naturalist's guidebook to owls, a worldwide look at the family, and an examination of the Near-Death Experience.

Of blue-blooded Southern stock through his Kentucky, Tennessee, Virginia, West Virginia, and North Carolina ancestors, he is a direct descendant of European royalty via his 6th great-grandfather, the Earl of Oxford, after which London's famous Harley Street is named. Among his celebrated male Celtic ancestors is Robert the Bruce, King of Scotland, Seabrook's 22nd great-grandfather. The 21st great-grandson of Edward I "Longshanks" Plantagenet), King of England, Seabrook is a thirteenth-generation Southerner through his descent from the colonists of Jamestown, Virginia (1607).

(Photo © Lochlainn Seabrook)

The 2nd, 3rd, and 4th great-grandson of dozens of Confederate soldiers, one of his closest connections to Lincoln's War is through his 3rd great-grandfather, Elias Jent, Sr., who fought for the Confederacy in the Thirteenth Cavalry Kentucky under Seabrook's 2nd cousin, Colonel Benjamin E. Caudill. The Thirteenth, also known as "Caudill's Army," fought in numerous conflicts, including the Battles of Saltville, Gladsville, Mill Cliff, Poor Fork, Whitesburg, and Leatherwood.

Seabrook is a direct descendant of the families of Alexander H. Stephens, John Singleton Mosby, William Giles Harding, and Edmund Winchester Rucker, and is related to the following Confederates and other 18th- and 19th-Century luminaries: Robert E. Lee, Stephen Dill Lee, Stonewall Jackson, Nathan Bedford Forrest, James Longstreet, John Hunt Morgan, Jeb Stuart, Pierre G. T. Beauregard (approved the Confederate Battle Flag design), George W. Gordon, John Bell Hood, Alexander Peter Stewart, Arthur M. Manigault, Joseph Manigault, Charles Scott Venable, Thornton A. Washington, John A. Washington, Abraham Buford, Edmund W. Pettus, Theodrick "Tod" Carter, John B. Womack, John H. Winder, Gideon J. Pillow, States Rights Gist, Henry R. Jackson, John Lawton Seabrook, John C. Breckinridge, Leonidas Polk, Zachary Taylor, Sarah Knox Taylor (first wife of Jefferson Davis), Richard Taylor, Davy Crockett, Daniel Boone, Meriwether Lewis (of the Lewis and Clark Expedition) Andrew Jackson, James K. Polk, Abram Poindexter Maury (founder of Franklin, TN),

Zebulon Vance, Thomas Jefferson, Edmund Jennings Randolph, George Wythe Randolph (grandson of Jefferson), Felix K. Zollicoffer, Fitzhugh Lee, Nathaniel F. Cheairs, Jesse James, Frank James, Robert Brank Vance, Charles Sidney Winder, John W. McGavock, Caroline E. (Winder) McGavock, David Harding McGavock, Lysander McGavock, James Randal McGavock, Randal William McGavock, Francis McGavock, Emily McGavock, William Henry F. Lee, Lucius E. Polk, Minor Meriwether (husband of noted pro-South author Elizabeth Avery Meriwether), Ellen Bourne Tynes (wife of Forrest's chief of artillery, Captain John W. Morton), South Carolina Senators Preston Smith Brooks and Andrew Pickens Butler, and famed South Carolina diarist Mary Chesnut.

Seabrook's modern day cousins include: Patrick J. Buchanan (conservative author), Cindy Crawford (model), Shelby Lee Adams (Letcher Co., Kentucky, photographer), Bertram Thomas Combs (Kentucky's 50th governor), Edith Bolling (wife of President Woodrow Wilson), and actors Andy Griffith, George C. Scott, Robert Duvall, Reese Witherspoon, Lee Marvin, Rebecca Gayheart, and Tom Cruise.

Seabrook's screenplay, *A Rebel Born*, based on his book of the same name, has been signed with acclaimed filmmaker Christopher Forbes (of Forbes Film). It is now in pre-production, and is set for release in 2017 as a full-length feature film. This will be the first movie ever made of Nathan Bedford Forrest's life story, and as a historically accurate project written from the Southern perspective, is destined to be one of the most talked about Civil War films of all time.

Born with music in his blood, Seabrook is an award-winning, multi-genre, BMI-Nashville songwriter and lyricist who has composed some 3,000 songs (250 albums), and whose original music has been heard in film (*A Rebel Born, Cowgirls 'n Angels, Confederate Cavalry, Billy the Kid: Showdown in Lincoln County, Vengeance Without Mercy, Last Step, County Line, The Mark*) and on TV and radio worldwide. A musician, producer, multi-instrumentalist, and renown performer—whose keyboard work has been variously compared to pianists from Hargus Robbins and Vince Guaraldi to Elton John and Leonard Bernstein—Seabrook has opened for groups such as the Earl Scruggs Review, Ted Nugent, and Bob Seger, and has performed privately for such public figures as President Ronald Reagan, Burt Reynolds, Loni Anderson, and Senator Edward W. Brooke. Seabrook's cousins in the music business include: Johnny Cash, Elvis Presley, Billy Ray and Miley Cyrus, Patty Loveless, Tim McGraw, Lee Ann Womack, Dolly Parton, Pat Boone, Naomi, Wynonna, and Ashley Judd, Ricky Skaggs, the Sunshine Sisters, Martha Carson, and Chet Atkins.

Seabrook lives with his wife and family in historic Middle Tennessee, the heart of Forrest country and the Confederacy, where his conservative Southern ancestors fought valiantly against Liberal Lincoln and the progressive North in defense of Jeffersonianism, constitutional government, and personal liberty.

LOCHLAINNSEABROOK.COM

If you enjoyed this book you will be interested in Colonel Seabrook's other popular related titles:

☞ EVERYTHING YOU WERE TAUGHT ABOUT THE CIVIL WAR IS WRONG, ASK A SOUTHERNER!
☞ EVERYTHING YOU WERE TAUGHT ABOUT AMERICAN SLAVERY IS WRONG, ASK A SOUTHERNER!
☞ CONFEDERATE FLAG FACTS: WHAT EVERY AMERICAN SHOULD KNOW ABOUT DIXIE'S SOUTHERN CROSS
☞ CONFEDERACY 101: AMAZING FACTS YOU NEVER KNEW ABOUT AMERICA'S OLDEST POLITICAL TRADITION

Available from Sea Raven Press and wherever fine books are sold

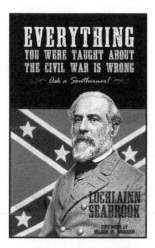
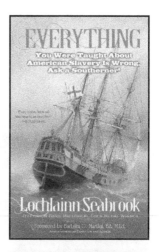

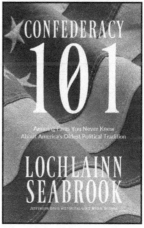

ALL OF OUR BOOK COVERS ARE AVAILABLE AS 11" X 17" POSTERS, SUITABLE FOR FRAMING.

SeaRavenPress.com • NathanBedfordForrestBooks.com

CPSIA information can be obtained
at www.ICGtesting.com
Printed in the USA
JSHW020630100822
29113JS00003B/216